Artificial Intelligence: Foundations, Theory, and Algorithms

Series editors
Barry O'Sullivan
Cork, Ireland

Michael Wooldridge
Oxford, United Kingdom

More information about this series at http://www.springer.com/series/13900

Justyna Petke

Bridging Constraint Satisfaction and Boolean Satisfiability

 Springer

Justyna Petke
Dept. of Computer Science
University College London
London, United Kingdom

Artificial Intelligence: Foundations, Theory, and Algorithms
ISBN 978-3-319-37364-5   ISBN 978-3-319-21810-6   (eBook)
DOI 10.1007/978-3-319-21810-6

Springer Cham Heidelberg New York Dordrecht London

Printed on acid-free paper

Springer International Publishing AG Switzerland is part of Springer Science+Business Media (www.springer.com)

Preface

A wide range of problems can be formalized as a set of constraints that need to be satisfied. In fact, such a model is called a constraint satisfaction problem (CSP). Another way to represent a problem is to express it as a formula in propositional logic, or, in other words, a Boolean satisfiability problem (SAT). In the quest to find efficient algorithms for solving instances of CSP and SAT specialised software has been developed. It is, however, not clear when should we choose a SAT-solver over a constraint solver (and vice versa). CSP-solvers are known for their domain-specific reasoning, whereas SAT-solvers are considered to be remarkably fast on Boolean instances. In this book we tackle these issues by investigating the connections between CSP and SAT.

In order to answer the question why SAT-solvers are so efficient on certain classes of CSP instances, we first present the various ways one can encode a CSP instance into SAT. Next, we show that with some encodings SAT-solvers simulate the effects of enforcing a form of local consistency, called k-consistency, in expected polynomial-time. Thus SAT-solvers are able to solve CSP instances of bounded-width structure efficiently in contrast to conventional constraint solvers. By considering the various ways one can encode CSP domains into SAT, we give theoretical reasons for choosing a particular SAT encoding for several important classes of CSP instances. In particular, we show that with this encoding many problem instances that can be solved in polynomial-time will still be easily solvable once they are translated into SAT. Furthermore, we show that this is not true for several other encodings.

Finally, we compare the various ways one can use a SAT-solver to solve the classical problem of the pigeonhole principle. We perform both theoretical and empirical comparison of the various encodings. We conclude that none of the known encodings for the classical representation of the problem will result in an efficiently solvable SAT instance. Thus in this case constraint solvers are a much better choice.

Acknowledgements

This book arose from my DPhil thesis 'On the Bridge Between Constraint Satisfaction and Boolean Satisfiability' awarded by the University of Oxford in 2012.

First and foremost I would like to thank my supervisor Peter Jeavons for his enthusiastic encouragement and valuable guidance throughout my doctorate studies. I could not have imagined having a better supervisor.

I thank my colleagues from the Oxford Constraints group: Stanislav Živný, András Salamon, Christopher Jefferson, Karen Petrie, Páidí Creed, Evgenij Thorstensen, Conrad Drescher, Markus Aschinger as well as David Cohen. I would also like to thank my college advisor Joël Ouaknine.

I am especially thankful to Stanislav Živný with whom I shared an office throughout my doctoral studies. I am grateful for his advice and encouragement.

I would also like to thank my examiners, Georg Gottlob and Barry O'Sullivan, for providing helpful corrections as well as my former supervisor Robin Hirsch and Daniel Hulme for getting me in touch with the Oxford Constraints group in the first place.

The provision of a Doctoral Training Award by the UK Engineering and Physical Sciences Research Council is greatly appreciated. I am also grateful to the Department of Computer Science and St John's College, Oxford, for financial support.

Finally, I would like to thank my family and friends. My parents and grandparents have been a constant source of support and this book and the related thesis would certainly not have existed without them.

Contents

List of Figures

Chapter 1
Introduction

These little grey cells. It is up to them.

Agatha Christie

Very often in science ideas emerge that are later to be found very similar or even equivalent, just named differently. At other times a more abstract concept gets defined that is an umbrella for a well-known set of things. It seems that the story of *constraint satisfaction* and *Boolean satisfiability* follows these two paths. These two areas of knowledge developed separately. However, the Boolean satisfiability problem (SAT) can be viewed as a subset of the general constraint satisfaction problem (CSP). The implications of this realization have only been studied after extensive research has been done into the two branches of knowledge. Hence, certain connections are yet to be discovered. This book investigates this *bridge* between *constraint satisfaction* and *Boolean satisfiability*.

So, what does *constraint satisfaction* deal with? What is a constraint? What are the applications of *Boolean satisfiability*? How are CSP instances and SAT formulae solved? Which techniques are used in constraint solvers? What methods do modern SAT-solvers implement? Answers to all these questions can be found in Chapter 2. A short history of SAT and CSP as well as various definitions used throughout this book are also presented in this chapter.

Because of the similarities between constraint satisfaction problems and Boolean satisfiability problems, SAT-solvers can be used to solve various CSP instances. Hence, given a constraint problem, one has a wide range of solvers to choose from, coming from both research areas. In order to check how the two types of solvers perform, we choose a few standard ones and test those on a well-defined sets of instances in Chapter 3. Even though SAT can be viewed as a subset of CSP and thus translating into SAT might not seem like a good idea, especially if the instances have large domains, SAT-solvers are considered to be extremely efficient. Therefore, sometimes the speed-up in solver performance outweighs the translation effort. Some examples of this are shown in Chapter 3.

© Springer International Publishing Switzerland 2015
J. Petke, *Bridging Constraint Satisfaction and Boolean Satisfiability*,
Artificial Intelligence: Foundations, Theory, and Algorithms,
DOI 10.1007/978-3-319-21810-6_1

In order to use any problem solving framework one must formulate a problem within that framework. Frequently this first decision has a huge impact on the efficiency of finding a solution. This is especially true in computer science, as one can obtain significantly different runtimes for the same algorithm depending on the model used — these may even change from milliseconds to centuries. Suppose we have a set of one million variables that need to be assigned values from the range $[1, 1000000]$ in an ascending order such that no two variables are assigned the same value. This problem has a trivial solution where variable 1 is assigned value 1, variable 2 is assigned value 2, etc. Suppose we have an algorithm that reads a variable and assigns it the lowest value that satisfies the constraints. If the problem is formulated in such a way that variable 1 is read first, variable 2 second, etc., then the proposed algorithm will solve it immediately. However, if the variables are entered in reverse order, the algorithm will have to perform additional work in order to find a solution. It will examine many possible partial solutions that cannot be completed. It is therefore not surprising that in some cases the time to find a solution may rise from seconds to hours even on the fastest computer, depending on the problem representation.

In Chapter 4 we describe the various ways in which a constraint problem can be modelled as a SAT formula. In particular, we present different approaches for encoding the domains and constraints of CSP instances. In this chapter we also try to answer the questions: What are the desirable properties of a SAT encoding? Could those be precisely identified? What should be regarded as a *good* encoding?

One desirable feature of a SAT encoding is investigated in Chapter 5, namely the existence of a short refutation of a particular type. In that chapter we establish a connection between this desirable property of a SAT formula and a certain central concept in the study of constraint satisfaction problems. We also relate this feature to the performance of a SAT-solver. Finally, by using these two results, we provide an answer to the question why SAT-solvers are so efficient on certain families of CSP instances. This result sheds some light onto the long-standing question about the remarkable efficiency of modern Boolean satisfiability solvers.

Following on the question of how to model CSP instances as SAT formulae, certain classes of CSP instances are considered in Chapter 6. These are known to be easily solvable by using standard CSP solving techniques. In this chapter we check whether such problem instances will be solved quickly using SAT-solvers by considering the various ways one can translate a constraint problem into SAT. In particular, we investigate the impact of encoding CSP domains on the complexity of the resultant formulae. As a result we provide an explanation why Boolean satisfiability solvers perform so well on a certain SAT encoding of instances belonging to specific CSP classes. Moreover, we provide complexity results for constraint solvers on the instances of the CSP classes considered.

Given all the theoretical results about SAT encodings and solver performance in the previous chapters we apply our findings to a concrete problem in Chapter 7. We consider the famous pigeonhole problem, that is the problem of arranging n pigeons into $n - 1$ holes without putting more than one pigeon in any hole. We provide a theoretical explanation for the behaviour of SAT-solvers on various encodings of the problem and perform an experimental evaluation. Furthermore, we evaluate the strength of our theoretical findings against results obtained in practice.

The main contributions of this book are summarised in Chapter 8, which provides a summary of the results obtained as well as some open questions and future research directions.

Chapter 2
Background

> *Words, mademoiselle, are only the outer clothing of ideas.*
> Agatha Christie

Both constraint satisfaction and Boolean satisfiability problems have been around for centuries. However, the terms were only coined in the twentieth century. Boolean satisfiability has its roots in logic. In fact, any propositional logic formula is an instance of the *Boolean satisfiability problem* (SAT). That's why the terms *propositional satisfiability* or simply just *satisfiability* are also commonly used. Constraint satisfaction, on the other hand, belongs to the field of artificial intelligence. It covers a very wide range of problems. Graph colouring, *n*-queens and time scheduling are just a few examples of problems which can be modelled as a set of *constraints* that need to be satisfied. *Constraint programming* (CP) deals with solving these kinds of problems.

Boolean satisfiability and constraint satisfaction independently emerged as new fields of computer science and significantly different approaches have been used to solve problems in these two areas of knowledge. Interestingly enough, any propositional formula can actually be viewed as an instance of the *constraint satisfaction problem* (CSP), so SAT can be seen as a special case of CSP (for a comprehensive overview on the history of CSP and SAT see [FM06] and [FM09]).

In this chapter we review algorithms used for solving instances of CSP and SAT. Section 2.1 introduces the constraint satisfaction problem. Section 2.2 presents the most common algorithms used in standard constraint solvers; variations on the basic propagation and search strategies are also discussed. Section 2.3 introduces the Boolean satisfiability problem. Section 2.4 deals with the methods used in SAT-solvers. Section 2.5 considers hybrid approaches and Section 2.6 concludes the chapter.

© Springer International Publishing Switzerland 2015
J. Petke, *Bridging Constraint Satisfaction and Boolean Satisfiability*,
Artificial Intelligence: Foundations, Theory, and Algorithms,
DOI 10.1007/978-3-319-21810-6_2

2.1   Constraint satisfaction problem (CSP)

Any problem that needs to satisfy a set of *constraints* (also known as *relations*) between variables having finite domains is in fact an instance of the (finite-domain) *constraint satisfaction problem* (CSP) which is formally defined as follows.

Definition 2.1 (CSP) *An instance of the* constraint satisfaction problem (CSP) *is specified by a triple* (V, D, C), *where*

- *V is a finite set of* variables;
- $D = \{D_v \mid v \in V\}$ *where each set D_v is the set of possible values for the variable v, called the* domain *of v;*
- *C is a finite set of* constraints. *Each constraint in C is a pair (R_i, S_i) where*

  - *S_i is an ordered list of m_i variables, called the constraint* scope;
  - *R_i is a relation over D of arity m_i, called the constraint* relation.

A simple example of a CSP instance is the 8-queens problem: one needs to place 8 queens on a 8×8 chessboard in such a way that no two queens attack each other. In this case queens can be regarded as variables, positions on the chessboard as domain values and constraints are the restrictions specifying that no two queens share the same row, column or diagonal (see Figure 2.1).

It is worth mentioning that in theoretical papers D often denotes a single set of domain values. In that context, to express that a variable v can only take values from some subset of D, unary constraints are introduced. In practice, however, CSP-solvers usually work by maintaining a list of available values for each variable and removing the unsatisfiable variable-value pairs. For this purpose, the above definition is more suitable.

Definition 2.2 *A solution to a CSP instance $P = (V, D, C)$ is an assignment of values from D to each of the variables in V, which satisfies all of the constraints in C simultaneously. Formally, a solution is a map $h : v \in V \to \bigcup D_v$ such that $h(v) \in D_v$, for all $v \in V$, and $h(S_i) \in R_i$, for all i, where the expression $h(S_i)$ denotes the result of applying h to the tuple S_i, coordinate-wise (in other words, if $S_i = (v_1, \cdots, v_k)$, then $h(S_i) = (h(v_1), \cdots, h(v_k))$).*

Fig. 2.1 An example solution to the 8-queens problem.

A CSP is called binary if each constraint scope includes exactly two variables. Any binary CSP can be represented as a constraint graph, in which each node corresponds to a variable and each edge represents a constraint between two nodes.

Definition 2.3 *Each node in the* primal graph *of a (binary) CSP instance P represents a variable of P. Two nodes are connected by an edge if and only if they are in the scope of the same constraint.*

Note that any non-binary CSP can be transformed into an equivalent binary CSP [RDP91]. Hence any CSP can be represented as a constraint graph[1]. In an *ordered* constraint graph the vertices are arranged in a linear order.

Definition 2.4 *[Fre82] The width of a vertex in an ordered constraint graph is the number of edges that lead back from that vertex to its predecessors (in the linear order). The width of an ordered constraint graph is the maximum width of any of its vertices. The* width of a constraint graph *is the minimum width of all the orderings of that graph.*

Definition 2.5 *[Dec06, Def. 7.10] The induced width of an ordered constraint graph is the width of the induced ordered graph, obtained by processing the vertices recursively, from last to first; when vertex v is processed, all its earlier neighbours are connected. The* tree-width[2] *of a graph is the minimal induced width over all its orderings.*

Let us now introduce another way by which one can represent a CSP instance graphically.

Definition 2.6 *Each node in the* incidence graph *of a CSP instance P represents either a variable or a constraint of P. Two nodes are connected by an edge if and only if one of them represents a constraint C and the other a variable in the scope of C.*

Moreover, we can translate a non-binary CSP into a binary one using the *hidden variable* method [RDP91].

Definition 2.7 *Let $P = (V, D, C)$ be a CSP instance. For each constraint $C_i \in C$ introduce a new variable v_{C_i} with domain D_{C_i} of tuples t satisfying C_i. Let $V' = V \cup \{v_{C_i} \mid C_i \in C\}$, $D' = D \cup \bigcup_{C_i \in C} D_{C_i}$ and $C' = \{v_{C_i} = t \leftrightarrow \forall_{t_j \in t} v_j = t_j$*

---

[1]It is worth mentioning, however, that sometimes the binary representation of a non-binary CSP needs to introduce new nodes or edges. For instance, consider the not-all-equal constraint on three variables. This is a ternary constraint and cannot be represented by a constraint graph with three nodes representing the original variables and edges representing binary constraints on these variables. Because of those often extensive additional space requirements, and the loss of information about the problem structure, the method of translating a non-binary CSP instance into a binary one is not usually used in practice.

[2]An alternative definition of tree-width was given in [RS86], where the concept was first introduced.

$| \ t \in D_{C_i} \wedge v_j \in V\}$, where v_j represents the jth variable in the scope of C_i. Then $P' = (V', D', C')$ is the hidden variable representation of P.

Note that the primal graph of the hidden variable representation of P is the incidence graph of P.

The structure of a non-binary CSP instance can be also represented by a hypergraph.

Definition 2.8 *A hypergraph is a pair $H = (V, E)$, where V is an arbitrary set, called the vertices of H, and E is a set of subsets of V, called the hyperedges of H.*

For any CSP instance, the scopes of all the constraints can be viewed as the hyperedges of an associated hypergraph whose vertices are the variables.

2.2   CSP-solvers

An important implementation decision that creators of constraint solvers must make is the choice of an input format. There exists no standard modelling language. In the CSP-solver competitions benchmark instances are represented in the XML format [vDLR06, vDLR08]. However, higher-level modelling languages such as Zinc [NSB+07] and Essence [FGJ+07] have been developed in the quest to find a more expressive and succinct model for CSP input.

Example 2.9 *The 8-queens problem can be specified in Essence as follows:*

```
language ESSENCE 1.2.0

$ Index: column and row indices
letting Index be domain int(*1..8*)

$ arrangement: one queen is placed on each row,
$              at the column index specified by
$              this function; the bijection ensures
$              each column contains exactly one queen
find arrangement : function Index -> (*bijective*) Index

$ no queens share diagonals; neq stands for 'not equal'
such that forall q1, q2 : Index . q1 neq q2 implies
                |arrangement(q1) - arrangement(q2)| neq |q1 - q2|
```

The objective of a constraint solver is to find an assignment of variables such that the set of constraints imposing conditions on those variables is satisfied. One can identify two components in the algorithm underlying any constraint solver — *inference* (also called problem reduction) and *search*. Inference reduces the size of the search space which is then traversed in order to find a solution. It is usually done using *constraint propagation* and is interleaved with search.

2.2.1 Search

The simplest way to solve a CSP instance is to systematically generate all possible variable assignments and check if a particular combination of variables and values satisfies all the constraints. The algorithm stops either when such an assignment has been found or when all possible assignments have been tested and they all failed to satisfy at least one constraint. This algorithm is very inefficient as in the worst case it needs to check m combinations of variables and values, where m is the size of the Cartesian product of all the variable domains.

A more efficient way of searching for a solution to a CSP instance is backtracking. In its most basic form, the variables are instantiated in a sequence. As soon as all the variables of any constraint are assigned, it is checked whether this constraint is satisfied by this particular instantiation. If it is not, the process goes back to the last variable that has been assigned that has untried values and re-assigns another value to it. This can result in a much smaller number of assignments being considered. Unfortunately, the average complexity of backtracking still tends to be exponential in the number of variables [Kum92].

Several improvements on the basic backtrack algorithm have been developed. These include the so-called *look-back* methods [Bak95, GB65, FW92]. Backjumping is one of them. The principle behind this technique is that instead of re-assigning the most recently instantiated variable (that has untried values), a check is made to determine if it is better to re-instantiate another one which is higher up in the search tree. Let us give an example. Suppose the n variables $v_1, \ldots, v_{i-1}, v_i, v_{i+1}, \ldots v_n$ are instantiated sequentially and that v_{i+1} cannot be assigned whenever variable v_{i-1} gets assigned value 3. Suppose v_{i-1} is instantiated to 3. In the classic backtracking algorithm every possible value for variable v_i will be tested before the process backtracks to v_{i-1}. It would have been more efficient to backtrack directly to this variable. The purpose of backjumping is to find the best variable to be re-instantiated.

One of the backjumping techniques that has shown promising results is *conflict-directed backjumping* [CvB01, Pro93]. In this method a set of so-called conflicts is maintained for each variable: whenever an assignment of the current variable v_k is in conflict with an instantiation of a previous variable v_m, v_m is added to the conflict set of v_k. When every instantiation of v_k has failed, the process jumps back to the deepest variable in its conflict set, v_j. Simultaneously, v_ks conflict set (without v_j) is added to the conflict set of v_j and the search continues at v_j. This method provides some improvement on the classic backtracking algorithm, as on average fewer variable nodes are visited during search. However, this technique is not usually used in standard CSP-solvers. The so-called *look-ahead* methods involving constraint propagation (see Section 2.2.2) are more common as they are simpler to implement and, for instance, the Maintaining Arc Consistency algorithm (MAC) has been shown to be an efficient alternative to the backjumping algorithms [LBH04].

Another idea for boosting backtrack performance is by using *restarts with nogood recording* [LSTV07]. This so-called *look-back* technique was originally introduced in SAT-solvers. First, the number of maximum allowed backtracks is set. Let it be *m*. If during search *m* backtracks occur, the process is restarted with a different random variable ordering and the algorithm records a list of *nogoods*, that is instantiations of a subset of CSP variables that are not part of any solution [DF02]. Nogood recording prevents the search from traversing the same unsatisfiable search path twice. This technique was implemented in the Abscon 109 solver [LT06, LSTV07] which took part in the 2nd International CSP Solver Competition [vDLR06] and was in the top five in every category.

The order in which variables are chosen during search has a great impact on the efficiency of backtracking algorithms. One can distinguish static and dynamic variable orderings. A *static variable ordering* is usually chosen at the beginning of search and, as the name suggests, does not change during propagation. For example, variables may be ordered by the number of constraints they participate in, called their *degree*, either at the beginning of search or at the current state of search. These approaches are referred to as *degree-based orderings*. Variables may also be chosen for assignment in such a way that minimizes the width of a constraint graph [Fre82].

One of the most popular dynamic variable ordering heuristics orders variables according to the current size of their domains (*dom*) [HE80]. The variable with the smallest set of untried values is chosen first as it is most likely to fail. Other heuristics have also been proposed over the years, like *dom/deg* [FD95] which takes current domain sizes and variables' original degrees into account. None of the heuristics clearly outperforms the others, but dynamic variable orderings have generally been found to be more efficient in practice [BHLS04].

Whenever a backtracking algorithm makes a variable-value decision and checks if it satisfies all the constraints, we say that it *branches* on that decision [HM05]. There are essentially three branching schemes used in practice. In *d*-way branching a single value a is picked for a variable v and that variable assignment is branched on. In 2-way branching we additionally branch on the disequality $v \neq a$. Another possibility is to branch on the inequalities of the form $v > a$ and $v \leq a$.

Another key issue that influences the performance of a constraint solver is the order in which values are chosen for variable assignment [MOQ11]. Several value orderings have been tested [FD95]. The results show that the *min-conflicts* value ordering heuristic is often the most efficient one. In this method for each value of the current variable a count is kept of the number of other variable instantiations with which it conflicts. The value with the lowest count is chosen first, as it is the least probable to cause a conflict in the future.

It is worth mentioning that there are also other, less popular search methods, aside from backtracking algorithms, that are used in modern CSP-solvers. These include local search algorithms, which generally do not guarantee to find a solution even if one exists, and so are incomplete (for an overview see [HT06]).

2.2.2 *Constraint propagation*

All backtrack methods suffer from thrashing [Kum92], that is, they often do some redundant work when search fails several times due to the same problem. One of the main reasons is the occurrence of various inconsistencies in constraint problems. Consider, for example, a CSP instance containing a variable with domain $D_v = \{1, 2, 3, \ldots, 100\}$ ($|D_v| = 100$) and a unary constraint on that variable enforcing it to have value 100. Now, assuming an increasing value ordering is used, the first 99 values will be tried (and found to be incompatible with the constraint) before the variable is assigned the value 100. That's why almost all CSP-solvers use some form of propagation to get rid of such inconsistencies and hence reduce the search space.

In the theoretical literature problem reduction is often referred to as *consistency maintenance* or propagation [Tsa93]. The idea of using *local consistency* techniques to prune the search space is one of the oldest and most central ideas in constraint programming [Bes06]. It was introduced in 1974 by Montanari [Mon74]. Three years later Mackworth [Mac77] proposed algorithms for node-, arc- and path-consistencies which we present below.

The example we have just described lacks *node-consistency* which is defined as follows.

Definition 2.10 *A variable v is said to be node-consistent if and only if every unary constraint on v is satisfied by all $a \in D_v$.*

The algorithm for achieving node-consistency is very simple: one just needs to reduce the domain of each variable to the values that satisfy every unary constraint on that variable. In the example above, by enforcing node-consistency the first 99 values are removed from the domain of the variable in question before the search is started. Hence, the variable is instantiated to 100 immediately.

Another type of inconsistency that may arise is lack of *arc-consistency* as defined below.

Definition 2.11 *A variable v_i is said to be arc-consistent with another variable v_j if and only if for every value $a \in D_{v_i}$ there exists a value $b \in D_{v_j}$ such that the tuple (a, b) satisfies all binary constraints between v_i and v_j.*

Note that in Definition 2.11 above, if variable v_i is arc-consistent with variable v_j it does not necessarily mean that v_j is arc-consistent with v_i. Consider, for example, a CSP instance with two variables v_1 and v_2 with domains $\{1\}$ and $\{1, 2\}$ and a constraint $v_1 \neq v_2$. v_1 is arc-consistent with v_2 as for every assignment of v_1 there exists an assignment of v_2 that satisfies the constraint. However, v_2 is not arc-consistent with v_1, as for $v_2 = 1$ there is no valid value in the domain of v_1.

The most famous algorithm for achieving arc-consistency is AC3 [Mac77] presented in Algorithm 2.1. In this algorithm the REVISE procedure deletes values from the domain of variable v_i that would make edge (v_i, v_j) inconsistent in the constraint graph G. Procedure AC-3 ensures that all edges that are affected by such a deletion are checked for arc-consistency again. The algorithm has worst-case time complexity of $O(ed^3)$ where e is the number of edges and d is the largest domain size.

Algorithm 2.1 The AC-3 algorithm [Kum92].

---
procedure REVISE(v_i, v_j);
   DELETE ← false;
   for each x in D_i **do**
       if there is no y in D_j such that (x, y) is consistent, **then**
           delete x from D_i ;
           DELETE ← true;
       end if;
   end for;
   return DELETE;
end_REVISE
procedure AC-3
   $Q ← (v_i, v_j)$ in edges(G), $i \neq j$;
   while Q not empty **do**
       select and delete any edge (v_k, v_m) from Q;
       if REVISE(v_k, v_m), **then**
           $Q ← (v_i, v_k)$ such that (v_i, v_k) in edges(G), $i \neq k$, $i \neq m$
       end if;
   end while;
end_AC-3

Making a CSP instance arc-consistent does not immediately solve the problem, in general. Only if there is only one value left in every variable domain after making a constraint graph arc-consistent, then those values form a solution to the corresponding CSP. If the domain of some variable is empty, then the problem is unsatisfiable. If, however, some variable domain has size greater than 1, then one cannot be certain whether the CSP instance has a solution or not. Let $v \in CSP(V)$ be the variable that has values a_1 and a_2 in its domain after making the CSP arc-consistent. Let $v_1 \in CSP(V)$ and $v_2 \in CSP(V)$. It might be the case that v_1 is arc-consistent with v via value a_1 only and v_2 is arc-consistent with v via value a_2 only. Therefore for no fixed assignment of variable v is the CSP instance satisfiable.

Another form of inconsistency that may arise is a lack of *path-consistency* as defined below.

Definition 2.12 *A constraint graph is said to be* path-consistent *if and only if any pair of values allowed by the edge* (v_i, v_j) *is also allowed by all paths from* v_i *to* v_j. *A pair of values is allowed by a path from* v_i *to* v_j *if at every intermediate vertex values can be found that satisfy all the constraints along the path.*

Montanari [Mon74] presented an algorithm for enforcing path-consistency which was improved by Mackworth [Mac77]. Mohr and Henderson made further modifications [MH86] which were corrected by Han and Lee [HL88]. The algorithm they came up with has the worst-case time complexity of $O(n^3 d^3)$ where n is the number of variables and d is the largest domain size.

Several other algorithms achieving arc- and path-consistency have been proposed in the literature over the years. The most influential ones can be found in [Bes06].

Although enforcing path-consistency ensures a greater level of consistency than arc-consistency, it is still not sufficient for solving CSPs in general. Hence a question arises, if there exists a consistency enforcing algorithm that answers the question whether a CSP instance is satisfiable or not. Note that arc-consistency ensures consistency between any two nodes in the constraint graph that are connected by an edge, while path-consistency ensures consistency between any three such nodes. Hence the notion of consistency has been extended to k-consistency [Fre78, Coo89]. A formal definition is given below.

Definition 2.13 (k-consistency) *A constraint graph is said to be k-consistent if and only if any assignment of any set of $k - 1$ variables that satisfies all the constraints among these variables can be extended to a set of k variables that satisfies all the constraints among the k variables. A constraint graph is said to be strongly k-consistent if it is j-consistent $\forall j \leq k$.*

A strongly k-consistent constraint graph with k vertices has a solution which can be found immediately, as the following result indicates:

Theorem 2.14 *[Fre82] If a constraint graph is strongly j-consistent and $j > w$ where w is the width of the constraint graph, then a search order exists that is backtrack free.*

The time complexity of the optimal algorithm for achieving strong j-consistency is polynomial for any fixed j [Coo89]. The major drawback of making a constraint graph j-consistent for $j > 2$ is that, when running an algorithm for achieving the desired level of consistency, the width of the constraint graph may increase. Hence a higher level of consistency then needs to be achieved. This approach is very costly in terms of efficiency and hence it is not generally used in practice.

Till now we have only considered binary constraint graphs. However, the notion of consistency can be extended also to non-binary constraints.

The equivalent of arc-consistency for non-binary CSP instances is called *generalised-arc-consistency* (GAC) as defined below.

Definition 2.15 (GAC) *A variable v is said to be generalised-arc-consistent (GAC) with a constraint if and only if for every value $a \in D_v$ there exists an assignment of all the other variables of the constraint such that it is satisfied.*

Several algorithms for enforcing GAC have been developed. They are all based on some underlying arc-consistency algorithm [BR97, BRYZ05, GJMN07]. Some standard CSP-solvers that implement GAC include Minion [GJM06], Choco [CHOCOt08] and Abscon [LT06].

There are several other types of consistencies that are relatively cheap to achieve. These include singleton consistencies. The notion of a *singleton consistency* is general and applicable to all levels of consistency [PSW00].

Definition 2.16 ([PSW00]) *A problem is said to be* singleton arc-consistent *if and only if it has non-empty domains and for any instantiation of a variable, the resulting subproblem can be made arc-consistent with all domains non-empty.*

Definition 2.17 ([PSW00]) *A problem is said to be* generalised singleton arc-consistent *if and only if it has non-empty domains, and for any instantiation of a variable the resulting subproblem can be made generalised-arc-consistent with all domains non-empty.*

An algorithm for singleton consistency is as follows: first we enforce some level of consistency, then we test each instantiation of a variable for that consistency level. If a value is not singleton consistent, it is removed and the desired level of consistency is established again. This process is repeated until all values are singleton consistent [DB97, DB05]. Singleton arc-consistencies have been used, for instance, in the Abscon [LT06] and Casper [CBA05] constraint solvers.

In order to identify as quickly as possible which constraints need to be propagated the idea of *watched literals* has been introduced. The so-called *2-watched literals* scheme has been very successful in SAT (see Section 2.4). The CSP-solver Minion [GJM06] also takes advantage of watched literals. For instance, the Boolean sum constraint is solved using the following technique. If the constraint requires that at least c variables are constrained to take value 1, then $c + 1$ variables that still can be assigned value 1 are watched. Once one of these variables gets assigned to 0, another one is looked for. If none can be found, all watched variables are assigned 1. The good thing about watched literals, is that they are *backtrack-stable*. This means that the selection of variables being watched does not need to be changed when the algorithm backtracks.

Aside from constraint propagation, there are also other methods for reducing the search space. One of these is *symmetry breaking*. In many constraint problems one can find some symmetries. Consider, for instance, three variables v_1, v_2 and v_3 with domain D and constraints $v_1 \leq v_2$ and $v_1 \leq v_3$. Note that once it is detected that either v_2 or v_3 cannot be assigned some value, say $a \in D$, the other variable cannot take value a as well. Clearly, if more symmetries are involved, identifying them might significantly reduce the search space, as it suffices to propagate only one set of variables from each symmetrically equivalent class. The symmetry in the above example is called a variable symmetry, as there is a permutation of variables that leaves the CSP invariant [Pug05]. A permutation of values that leaves a given CSP invariant is called a value symmetry [Pug05]. These two symmetries are called *constraint symmetries*. *Solution symmetries* have also been identified [CJJ+06] and they preserve the set of solutions of a CSP instance. Symmetry breaking has been used, for instance, in the Choco [CHOCOt08] and the newest version of Abscon [LT06] constraint solvers.

2.2.3   Combining propagation and search

A major difference between the various algorithms used in CSP-solvers is the way and extent to which constraint propagation is incorporated into search. A desired level of consistency is achieved at first and then the search phase begins. Usually solvers enforce arc-consistency, so we will use this example to illustrate the solving process. Propagation is triggered on variable instantiation. Arc-consistency is established at that variable, that is, at the node in the search tree that corresponds to that variable. There are three scenarios afterwards: either the sizes of all the domain variables are equal to 1, or else some variable domain is empty, or else some variable domain size is greater than 1. In the first case we have found a solution. In the second case the variable instantiation that triggered propagation is invalid, so we backtrack and another value for that variable is tried. In the third case a new variable with domain size greater than 1 gets assigned which triggers propagation as before.

Until the mid-1990s it was believed that full arc-consistency would be too costly to achieve, so only partial arc-consistency was enforced during search. In 1994 Sabin and Freuder [SF94] showed that algorithms that establish full arc-consistency can be much more efficient, especially when solvers are run on hard problem instances. In modern constraint solvers usually each type of constraint has an associated propagation algorithm which achieves the desired level of consistency for that constraint.

2.3   Boolean satisfiability problem (SAT)

Definition 2.18 *The problem of deciding whether there is a variable assignment that satisfies a propositional formula is called the* Boolean satisfiability problem (SAT).

SAT is known to be NP-complete [Coo71]. However, SAT-solvers have been widely used in practice as they can often efficiently handle problems with thousands and sometimes even millions of variables [ZM02].

2.4   SAT-solvers

SAT-solvers generally input propositional formulae in the form of conjunctions of disjunctive clauses (CNF). The main advantage of using CNF as the standard form of solver input can easily be seen when testing problem instances that have no solution. Once some disjunctive clause is found to be unsatisfiable, then the whole problem becomes unsatisfiable. There is no need for further checks. Note that any propositional formula can be transformed into CNF in linear time by introducing auxiliary variables as long as the original formula contains Boolean operators that have linear clausal encodings [Pre09]. Such operators include $\wedge$ (*and*), $\vee$ (*or*), $\rightarrow$ (*implies*) and $\neg$ (*not*). Moreover, the standardised input format allows for quick and easy comparison of SAT-solvers.

As far as the solving techniques are concerned, modern standard SAT-solvers still use some variation of the algorithm developed by Davis, Putnam, Logemann and Loveland (DPLL) in the 1960s [DLL62, DP60]. The pseudo-code is shown in Algorithm 2.2, and the various subroutines mentioned are described in more detail below.

Algorithm 2.2 The DPLL algorithm [ZM02].

DPLL

```
    status = preprocess();
    if status ≠ UNKNOWN then
        return  status;
    end if;
    while true do                                                Decision
        make_branch_decision();
        while true do                                           Unit Propagation
            status = deduce();
            if status == INCONSISTENT then                      Conflict
                resolved = analyse_conflict_and_backtrack();
                if not resolved then
                    return  UNSATISFIABLE;
                end if;
            else if status == SOLUTION_FOUND then
                return  SATISFIABLE;
            else
                break;
            end if;
        end while;
    end while;
```

The aim of the pre-processing stage is to simplify the input formula. This usually means reducing the number of variables and adding some clauses. This can be done by using *propositional resolution* as defined below.

Definition 2.19 ([Rob65]) *The process of using a deduction rule to substitute* $(x \vee C_1) \wedge (\neg x \vee C_2)$ *with* $(C_1 \vee C_2)$, *where* C_1 *and* C_2 *are propositional clauses and* x *is a Boolean variable, is called* (propositional) resolution. *The resultant clause is called the* resolvent.

Resolution is known to be a refutation complete and sound proof system for CNF formulae.

Definition 2.20 *A resolution proof of a clause C from a set of initial clauses Φ is a sequence of clauses $C_1, C_2, \cdots, C_m$, where $C_m = C$ and each C_i follows by the resolution rule from some collection of clauses, each of which is either contained in*

Φ *or else occurs earlier in the sequence. If C_m is the empty clause, then we say that the derivation is a resolution proof (or refutation) of* Φ.

Another example of a simplification rule is the *pure literal rule* [GPFW96]. If a variable is never negated (that is occurs as a positive literal only) or is always negated (that is occurs as a negative literal only) then it can be assigned value *True* or *False* respectively, and hence all the clauses in which it occurs are satisfied. For instance, consider the two clauses $v_1 \vee \neg v_2$ and $v_1 \vee v_3$. v_1 occurs as a positive literal only, so it can immediately be assigned value *True*.

It is worth mentioning that simplification does not necessarily reduce the search space [LMS01]. Pre-processing also involves choosing an initial variable order. It turns out that randomisation at this stage often produces quite good results [GSK98].

2.4.1 Search

At the *make_branch_decision* stage a free variable is chosen for assignment. One of the most successful orderings is the Variable State Independent Decaying Sum (VSIDS) ordering used in the Chaff SAT-solver [MMZ$^+$01]. To implement this ordering, for each literal a count is kept of the number of unresolved clauses in which that literal occurs. When at the deduction stage clauses are added, the literal counts are increased accordingly. The variable that appears in the literal with the highest count is chosen for assignment. Branching heuristics based on literal count have widely been used since the 1990s and include the largest individual sum heuristic (DLIS) and its variations [MS99]. What VSIDS adds to the picture is periodically dividing all the counts by some constant number. This method gives priority to variables that constrain the biggest number of clauses and have been recently active.

The idea of *activity* has also been used in the BerkMin SAT-solver [GN02]. It uses a technique similar to VSIDS, additionally increasing the counts of literals appearing in a clause that evaluates to false under the current assignment.

Once a variable is chosen for assignment, a decision level is assigned to it. The decision level informs the solver at which stage of search the decision for that particular variable was made. For instance, any variable that has been assigned a value at the pre-processing stage will be assigned 0 (or Top) decision level. The first variable that gets picked for assignment will have decision level 1. It is worth mentioning that if any variable gets assigned at the propagation stage, it will be given the same decision level as the variable that caused that assignment. For instance, given current decision $x_1 = False$ and clause $x_1 \vee \neg x_2$, x_2 must be assigned value *False* for that clause to be satisfied. Hence if x_1 has decision level, say 5, so will x_2. More details on propagation will be given in the next section.

The symmetry breaking technique used in CSP-solvers has recently been applied to SAT-solvers. The symmetries here mean permutations of literals which do not change the CNF formula. They just re-arrange the clauses and literals within the clauses. Examples of SAT-solvers which exploit symmetry in CNF formulae include SymChaff [Sab05] and Shatter [AMS03].

2.4.2   *Boolean constraint propagation (BCP)*

At the deduction stage of the DPLL algorithm, variables are assigned according to some implication rules, until a conflict or a solution is found. This process is known as *Boolean constraint propagation (BCP)* and is carried out by the *deduce* subroutine in Algorithm 2.2.

The one rule that all SAT-solvers use is the *unit propagation rule* (or unit resolution):

Definition 2.21 (unit propagation) *The* unit propagation rule *states that if all but one literals in a clause evaluate to false under a partial assignment, then the last free literal has to be true. Such a clause is called a* unit clause.

For instance, consider the clause $v_1 \vee \neg v_2 \vee v_3$ and partial assignment $v_1 = False$ and $v_2 = True$. Then v_3 must be assigned value *True* for the clause to be satisfied.

Definition 2.22 *A* conflicting clause *is a clause that evaluates to false under the current assignment.*

The aim of the Boolean constraint propagation (BCP) stage in a SAT-solver is to identify unit and conflicting clauses as soon as possible. As the BCP stage is the most time-consuming part of the DPLL algorithm [BHZ06], a lot of research has been devoted to improving it. One method is based on keeping the count of true and false literals for each clause. By knowing the clause size it is then easy to check whether after some variable assignment the clause becomes unit or conflicting. As this method requires many counters to be updated whenever a variable gets assigned, it is usually not the most efficient one.

In the last decade algorithms have been developed that use the observation that it suffices to keep track of only two non-false literals per clause. Note that as long as a clause contains two non-false literals then it is neither unit nor conflicting. One method uses head/tail lists [ZS00]. For each clause the first and last non-false literals are kept track of by using head and tail pointers respectively. Variable assignments that do not affect those literals or assign them value *True* do not trigger any action. Once one of the literals pointed to by one of the head or tail pointers evaluates to false, the next non-false literal is looked for. If one is found that is not pointed to by both head and tail pointers then the algorithm continues, if head pointer meets the tail pointer (or the other way round) then, depending on the value of the literal they point to, we get either a conflicting or unit clause. A drawback of this method is that when the solver performs backtracking, work is done to move back pointers to their original positions. This problem has been resolved in the Chaff solver [MMZ⁺01] which uses the so-called *watched literals*.

In the *2-watched literal* scheme pointers to any two non-false literals are kept for each clause. Each variable has two lists of pointers pointing to positive and negative watched literals corresponding to it. Again, once after some variable assignment any of the watched literals evaluates to false, another one is looked for in the clauses which contain that literal. If one is found that is different from the other watched literal, the process continues. If the only choice is the other watched literal, then it is set to *True* if it has not already been assigned that value. If no non-false literal is found, then the clause is conflicting. The good thing about this approach is that during backtracking the pointers are not changed. This is because the literals being watched are the last to be assigned to *False*, so at backtracking they will become unassigned and hence can still be watched.

2.4.3 *Conflict analysis*

The last phase of the SAT solving process is conflict analysis and backtracking. It may happen that under the current assignment and after the propagation stage all literals in a clause evaluate to false. We say that a conflict occurred. SAT-solvers use learning in order to prevent the same conflict from happening again after backtrack. At this stage the solver also tries to figure out to which decision level in the search the process should backtrack. The simplest method for solving conflicts is trying the other value for the variable that has been assigned most recently as it directly caused the conflict. If both values cause conflict, another value is tried for the variable that has been assigned just before the latest one. This method thus backtracks just one decision level up the search tree and hence is not the most efficient. The idea of "jumping back" more than one decision level up was first introduced in CSP-solvers. It has since been used in SAT-solvers such as GRASP [MSS96].

In modern SAT-solvers learning is used to analyse the current conflict. In order to resolve a conflict, one needs to know what caused it, that is, what was the trail of decisions that forced the last non-false literal in the conflicting clause to be unsatisfied. All variable assignment decisions, made both at the search stage and inferred during propagation, can be represented by a so-called *implication graph*. Nodes of an implication graph represent variable assignments. By each node the decision level of each assignment is kept. A directed edge is drawn from node x to y if the unit resolution rule implies that assignment y must be *True* given x. Consider the clauses $v_4 \vee \neg v_2 \vee \neg v_1$, $v_6 \vee \neg v_3 \vee \neg v_5$, $v_5 \vee v_2$, $\neg v_2 \vee v_1$ and $v_4 \vee \neg v_2 \vee \neg v_1$. Suppose we first made a decision $v_4 = False$. Next, we assign $v_6 = False$ and then $v_3 = True$. The resulting implication graph is shown in Figure 2.2. Note that a conflict occurred at v_1, as once v_1 is assigned *True* by $\neg v_2 \vee v_1$, the clause $v_4 \vee \neg v_2 \vee \neg v_1$ evaluates to false. Once a conflicting clause is found under the current assignment, a so-called *conflict clause* is added to the problem.

Definition 2.23 *In the context of conflict analysis in SAT-solvers, a* conflict clause *is said to be a clause that can be deduced from the current conflict.*

Fig. 2.2 An example
implication graph.

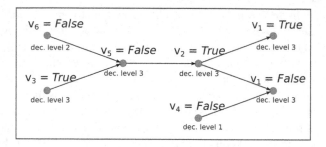

For instance, in the example described above, a conflict clause could be $v_5 \vee v_4$. Such a learned clause significantly helps prune the search space after backtrack. Frequently more than one conflict clause can be deduced from the current conflict. Hence some sort of selection strategy needs to be used.

Single assignments at the current decision level that imply current conflict are called *Unit Implication Points* (UIPs) [BHZ06]. In other words, if conflict is reached at vertex y, then x is a UIP if and only if any path from the decision variable (that is a variable that is assigned at the search stage) of the decision level of x to y needs to go through x. For instance, there are three implication points in Figure 2.2, as a conflict occurs if at the current decision level either v_3 gets assigned *True* or v_5 gets assigned *False* or v_2 gets assigned *True*.

The most common selection strategy for choosing conflict clauses uses clauses that contain a variable that occurs in a UIP. As there may be several UIPs, a question arises which UIP to choose. Several learning heuristics have been tested and the so-called FirstUIP scheme often seems to be the best one [ZMMM01]. In this scheme a conflict clause is added that contains a variable corresponding to the UIP that is closest to the conflict. Moreover, such a clause must be an asserting clause as defined below:

Definition 2.24 *An asserting clause is a conflict clause that contains only one variable that is assigned at the current decision level.*

In the example from Figure 2.2 three asserting clauses could be derived: $\neg v_2 \vee v_4$, $v_5 \vee v_4$ and $\neg v_3 \vee v_6 \vee v_4$. In this case the first one would be added to the SAT instance being solved, as in the implication graph UIP $v_2 = False$ is the closest to the conflict. An example of a non-asserting clause would be: $\neg v_2 \vee v_5 \vee v_4$.

Finally, the algorithm backtracks to the decision level that is second-highest of all the literal decision levels in the *asserting clause*. Note that such a clause can always be found as at least the clause composed of all the decision assignments made so far is an asserting clause.

In order to describe in what way the asserting clauses are searched for, a definition of the *antecedent clause* needs to be introduced:

Definition 2.25 *The* antecedent clause, *in the context of conflict analysis used in SAT-solvers, is said to be the clause that directly triggered the latest assignment in* *the current clause and includes the variable contained in the literal that has been assigned last.*

Once a conflicting clause is found each literal is substituted with its antecedent clause. If the resulting clause is not an asserting one, each of its literals is again substituted with its antecedent clause. The process continues until an asserting clause is found.

During conflict resolution many clauses might be added. Hence SAT-solvers usually implement some mechanism for removing redundant conflict clauses. BerkMin [GN02] solver counts the number of conflicts each clause has been involved in recently. Another heuristic deletes clauses that contain many non-false literals [BS97].

2.5   Hybrid solvers and SMT-solvers

SAT-solvers can actually be used for deciding the satisfiability of CSP instances. Such SAT-based solvers first translate the input instance into SAT and then use a SAT-solver. We will call such solvers SAT-based constraint solvers. Since constraint solvers and SAT-solvers share so much in common, hybrid solvers have also been recently introduced. One approach is to implement some domain-specific reasoning within a SAT-solver, another one is to implement a SAT engine within a constraint solver. The two architectures are discussed in [FS09]. The second approach has been used, for instance, as an extension of the G12 constraint solver [FS09]. The first approach is seen in another type of solvers coming from the research area of *SAT Modulo Theories* (SMT) [NOT06].

SMT-solvers decide the satisfiability of a ground first-order logic formula with respect to a background theory. Examples of theories include the theory of integers, theory of arrays or bit vectors. The formula $v - w \leq 5 \vee \neg x \vee v = f(w)$ is an example SMT clause, where v, w and x are variables (with x Boolean), and f is some unspecified function. At the core of an SMT-solver is a SAT-solver. The *theory solvers* simply check if the current assignments are feasible and can infer new facts which are then encoded as new clauses and passed onto the SAT-solver. SMT-solvers have been very successful in solving problems from the areas of hardware and software verification [NOT06].

2.6   Summary

Since the 1960s a lot of research has been going on in the area of constraint satisfaction and Boolean satisfiability. This has led to the development of various algorithms trying to solve the general CSP and SAT problems. The most efficient ones combine search and propagation. In the case of constraint solvers, constraint propagation is the most significant part of the solving process, as most efficiency gains are achieved thanks to pruning the search space by applying propagation techniques. As far as SAT-solvers are concerned, unit propagation and conflict-directed learning play the most important roles.

There are many similar ideas used in both CSP and SAT-solvers. In both cases variable order has an impact on the solver performance [BHLS04, MMZ+01]. Some form of learning has been applied both in CSP (nogoods [LSTV07]) and SAT (conflicts [ZMMM01]). However, it is worth mentioning that the introduction of learning techniques into SAT had a major influence on improving solver performance, whereas it has not had such a huge impact on boosting CSP-solver runtimes. The idea of non-chronological backtracking used in CSP [Bak95, GB65] has also had its application in SAT [ZMMM01]. In the last few years the watched literals method has significantly boosted the performance of standard SAT-solvers [MMZ+01] and recently they have been applied in some constraint solvers [GJM06].

Although one can find many similarities between CSP and SAT-solvers, the translation of ideas between constraint satisfaction and Boolean satisfiability is not always obvious, if at all possible. One reason is that CSP contains a broad class of problems which includes SAT. CSPs are closer in their description to real-world problems. Moreover, most constraint solvers can be tuned, that is the user can choose a specific variable ordering or search strategy. SAT-solvers, on the other hand, typically act as a black box. This difference might have come about as there is no standardised input for CSP-solvers and they can model a broader set of problems than SAT. Hence some CSP solving algorithms take specific problem features into account. There exist algorithms whose sole purpose is efficiently solving a certain type of constraints, like the global cardinality constraint [QGLOvB05] or the so-called constraints of difference [Rég94].

Another difference between CSP and SAT-solvers is the impact of value order on their performance. It does not have that much significance in SAT-solvers as the variables can only take two values: *True* or *False*. Hence not much research has been done on which of those two values is worth trying first for a variable. Therefore it is hard to say what performance gain, if any, could be achieved if a particular value order were chosen.

Moreover, in the theoretical literature one might find some ideas for boosting solver performance that have not yet been implemented. For instance, most CSP-solvers do not investigate the underlying structure of an instance. One reason is that finding such a structure might be tricky and costly in terms of time and space, and hence outweigh the possible performance gains. Another reason is the way propagation is implemented in CSP-solvers. Constraints "talk to each other" through the domain. Essentially what a constraint solver does is remove unsatisfiable domain values. There is no way, with current solver architectures, of combining information from two or more constraints and determining the satisfiability of the problem based on their structure.

Throughout the years the core algorithm for SAT has been DPLL, while there is no such standardised algorithm for CSP. In the last few years CSP research has even focused on finding the best algorithms for particular constraints rather than on a general model for propagating all constraints [GJM06, NSB$^+$07].

Current SAT-solvers are considered to be extremely efficient. Hence some researchers have developed CSP to SAT translations and used a SAT-solver engine for dealing with CSPs. Such translations often produce huge SAT instances. Interestingly enough, such SAT-based solvers did quite well in CSP-solver competitions [vDLR09, vDLR08, vDLR06]. They even performed well on the problem instances containing highly structured so-called global constraints, which are said to be the natural domain of CSP-solvers.

Furthermore, because of these close connections between CSP and SAT, hybrid solvers have been developed. Moreover, the area of SMT solving tries to incorporate the best of the two worlds: domain-specific reasoning and fast SAT solving.

Summing up, in the quest to find efficient algorithms for CSP and SAT-solvers, two separate areas of research have developed, namely constraint satisfaction and Boolean satisfiability. Although there may be many differences in their approaches to problem solving, they both benefit from each others' findings and a thorough comparative study of the two areas might lead to further useful developments.

Chapter 3
Solver performance on tractable CSPs: empirical evaluation

The secret of getting ahead is getting started.

Agatha Christie

Software tools for solving finite domain constraint problems are now freely available from several groups around the world. Examples include the Gecode system developed in Germany and Sweden [Sch11], the G12 finite domain solver developed in Australia [NSB+07], and the Minion constraint solver developed in the UK [GJM06].

One way to drive performance improvements in constraint solvers, which has proved very successful in the SAT-solving community, is to develop challenging benchmark instances. This approach can also help to drive improvements in the robustness and flexibility of constraint-solving software. For example, several families of benchmark MiniZinc instances have been distributed with G12 [NSB+07] since version 0.7, and these have been used to compare the performance of various solvers, and to develop and test an alternative solver, FznTini [Hua08], based on translation to Boolean satisfiability.

How can suitable benchmark instances be obtained? One obvious source of benchmark instances is from practical applications such as scheduling and manufacturing process organisation; the G12 MiniZinc suite includes several examples of this kind, such as "nurse scheduling" problems and "car sequencing" problems. Another common source of benchmark instances is combinatorial problems such as puzzles and games; the G12 MiniZinc suite also includes several examples of this kind, such as "Golomb ruler" problems and "kakuro" puzzles.

In this chapter we suggest another important source of useful benchmark instances which has not yet been systematically explored: the theoretical study of constraint satisfaction. From the very beginning of the study of constraint programming there has been a strand of research which has focused on identifying features of constraint problems which make them tractable to solve [CCJ94, Dec92, DBvH99, Fre85] and this research has gathered pace recently with the discovery of some deep connections between constraint problems and algebra [Bod08, BKJ05, Bul06, BV08], logic [CKS01, DKV02, FV98], and graph and hypergraph theory [CJG08, Gro07].

© Springer International Publishing Switzerland 2015
J. Petke, *Bridging Constraint Satisfaction and Boolean Satisfiability*,
Artificial Intelligence: Foundations, Theory, and Algorithms,
DOI 10.1007/978-3-319-21810-6_3

This research has focused on two main ways in which imposing restrictions on a constraint problem can ensure that it can be tractably solved. The first of these is to restrict the forms of constraints which are allowed; these are sometimes known as *constraint language* restrictions. For example, it was shown in [CCJ94] that certain forms of arithmetic constraint introduced in the CHIP programming language [vHDT92] had a property which ensured that they could be efficiently solved no matter how they were combined. It was also shown in [CCJ94] that many other forms of constraints also had the same property and could also be combined arbitrarily whilst allowing an efficient solution algorithm. Since then many other classes of so-called tractable constraint languages have been identified, and a sophisticated algebraic theory has been developed which aims to distinguish tractable forms of constraints from those which can lead to intractable problems [BKJ05, BV08].

The second standard approach to identifying restrictions on constraint problems which ensure tractability has been to consider restrictions on the way in which the constraints overlap; these are sometimes referred to as *structural restrictions*. For example, it was shown in [Fre85] that binary constraint problems where the underlying graph of the constraints has bounded-width can be efficiently solved by choosing an appropriate variable ordering. For non-binary constraint problems, where each constraint may involve more than two variables, the underlying structure is a hypergraph, and certain structural conditions on this hypergraph can again be sufficient to ensure tractability, regardless of the forms of constraint imposed. For example, if this hypergraph is acyclic [DP89] or has a bounded degree of cyclicity [GJC94] or a bounded hypertree width [GLS00] then the resulting constraint problem has been shown to be tractable. A complete characterisation of the class of hypergraphs which lead to tractable constraint problems was obtained in [Gro07], for problem classes where the maximum arity of each constraint is bounded. However, some of these structural tractability results rely on the assumption that constraints are represented extensionally, by an explicit table of allowed tuples, and this assumption is often not satisfied in practical constraint problems, where constraints are often represented by special-purpose algorithms known as propagators. A theory of structural tractability for constraints represented by propagators was developed in [GJ08], and results in rather small tractable classes.

In this chapter we begin the process of translating from theoretical results in the literature to concrete families of instances of constraint problems. We obtain several families which are known to be efficiently solvable by simple algorithms, but which cause great difficulties for some existing constraint solvers. Moreover, we identify cases where SAT-based constraint solvers perform sometimes even orders of magnitude better than conventional CSP-solvers.

3.1 Preliminaries

The definition of the CSP (see Definition 2.1) says nothing about how the individual constraints are represented in the specification of a particular concrete instance. For example, constraint relations may be specified by explicitly listing all of the allowed tuples of values, or perhaps all of the disallowed tuples of values, or simply by naming a standard relation such as "all-different". Although it is generally not an issue that is considered in the theoretical literature, it is clearly an important issue in practice to decide how problem instances will be encoded for input to a constraint solver, and the lack of a common agreed standard in this area is one of the difficulties of developing widely accepted benchmarks.

As mentioned in Section 2.2, two proposed standard higher-level languages for specifying constraint problems in practice are Zinc [NSB+07] and Essence [FGJ+07]. However, both of these languages are considered too abstract and too general to be used directly as the input language for current constraint solvers, so they both have more restricted subsets which are more suitable for solver input: these are called MiniZinc and Essence'. There exists a software translation tool, called Tailor [GMR08], which converts from Essence' specifications to the input language for the Minion solver. Another software translation tool distributed with the G12 software [NSB+07], converts from MiniZinc to a more restricted language known as FlatZinc, that serves as the input language for the G12 finite domain solver. The FznTini solver, developed by Huang, transforms a FlatZinc file into standard SAT-solver format, called DIMACS CNF[1], and then uses a Boolean Satisfiability problem (SAT) solver, called TiniSAT, to solve the resulting SAT problem [Hua08].

Note that in the theoretical literature the CSP is generally formalised as a *decision problem*: the question associated with each instance is simply to decide whether a solution exists. In practice, of course, it is often more natural to consider the corresponding *search problem*, which asks us to find a solution if one exists. However, we note that for any class of CSP instances where we are allowed to add unary *constant constraints*, fixing the assignments for some individual variables, we can find a solution with at most $|V| \times |D|$ iterations of the decision algorithm by adding a new unary constant constraint and calling the decision algorithm again on each iteration [Coh04]. In the experimental results recorded here we ask the solvers to solve the search problem.

The time complexity of this search problem is at most exponential in the size of the input, since the size of the total search space for possible solutions is $|D|^{|V|}$. Moreover, if we assume that each constraint is represented in such a way that checking whether a given assignment satisfies a given constraint can be completed in polynomial-time, then CSP clearly belongs to the problem class NP, since an

---

[1]DIMACS CNF is the standard input format for encoding CNF formulae. For example, the clause $x_1 \lor x_2 \lor \neg x_3$ would be encoded as: 1 2 −3 0, where 0 marks the end of the clause.

assignment can be verified in polynomial-time in the size of the input. However, for certain restricted classes of instances it is possible to find a solution, or verify that no solution exists, in polynomial-time. Such restricted classes will be called *tractable*.

Definition 3.1 *A class of CSP instances will be called* tractable *if there exists an algorithm which finds a solution to all instances in that class, or reports that there are no solutions, whose time complexity is polynomial in the size of the instance specification.*

Many examples of tractable classes have been identified in the literature: see [PJ97] for an early survey, and [BV08, Gro06] for more recent surveys. In this chapter we will focus on some of the simplest and most widely known examples of tractable classes. In particular, we will construct families of instances that are tractable for each of the following reasons:

- All constraints allow some constant value d to be assigned to every variable (Section 3.2).
- All constraints are *max-closed constraints* as defined in [JC95] (Section 3.3).
- All constraints are *0/1/all constraints* as defined in [CCJ94] (Section 3.4).
- All constraints are *connected-row-convex* as defined in [DBvH99] (Section 3.5).
- The constraint hypergraph has bounded-width (Section 3.6).

3.2   Constant-closed constraints

Classes of CSP instances where each constraint allows some constant value d to be assigned to every variable are clearly tractable according to Definition 3.1 because they can be solved by the trivial algorithm that assigns the value d to every variable in the instance. Such classes were included (for completeness) in several early lists of tractable classes, including Schaefer's Dichotomy Theorem for the Boolean satisfiability problem [Sch78] and the first survey of tractable cases identified by the algebraic approach to constraint complexity [JCG97].

Surprisingly, instances with this property do occur in practice: the majority of the satisfiable binary decision diagram instances used in the third CSP-solver competition [vDLR08] have constant solutions[2].

To investigate whether the presence of a constant solution affects the performance of standard constraint solvers we generated CSP instances with just one solution — the constant one. Our instance generator took as input the number of variables, n, and the number of possible values for each variable, d and created instances with n

---

[2]This observation was made by Marc van Dongen in a personal communication.

MiniZinc   Essence'

```
array[1..4] of var 0..4: X;    language ESSENCE' 1.b.a
constraint                     letting D be domain int(1..4)
(                              find X : matrix indexed by [D]
((X[1] = 1)/\(X[2] = 0))                            of int(0..4)
\/((X[1] = 0)/\(X[2] = 0))     such that
\/((X[1] = 2)/\(X[2] = 2))     (
) /\ (                         ((X[1] = 1)/\(X[2] = 0))
((X[2] = 0)/\(X[3] = 0))       \/((X[1] = 0)/\(X[2] = 0))
\/((X[2] = 0)/\(X[3] = 1))     \/((X[1] = 2)/\(X[2] = 2))
\/((X[2] = 2)/\(X[3] = 2))     ) /\ (
) /\ (                         ((X[2] = 0)/\(X[3] = 0))
((X[3] = 3)/\(X[4] = 1))       \/((X[2] = 0)/\(X[3] = 1))
\/((X[3] = 4)/\(X[4] = 1))     \/((X[2] = 2)/\(X[3] = 2))
\/((X[3] = 2)/\(X[4] = 2))     ) /\ (
) ;                            ((X[3] = 3)/\(X[4] = 1))
solve satisfy;                 \/((X[3] = 4)/\(X[4] = 1))
                               \/((X[3] = 2)/\(X[4] = 2))
                               )
```

Fig. 3.1 Typical constant-closed CSP instance specifications generated in MiniZinc and Essence' for $n = 4$ and $d = 5$. All constraints allow the value 2 for all variables.

variables each with domain $0, \ldots, (d-1)$. Each of the generated constraints allowed the value $\lfloor d/2 \rfloor$ to be assigned to all variables[3].

As a simple way to ensure that each instance had only this solution, we generated a line of binary constraints, with one constraint on each successive pair of variables. On the first $n - 1$ variables these constraints were obtained by choosing a random list of $d/2$ allowed values for each variable (with repetitions) from the domain $0 \ldots (d/2)$ and allowing just those pairs of values formed by the corresponding entries in two successive lists (together with the pair $(\lfloor d/2 \rfloor, \lfloor d/2 \rfloor)$). The final binary constraint, between the $(n - 1)^{th}$ and n^{th} variables, restricted the $(n - 1)^{th}$ variable to values in the other half of the domain, thus eliminating all possible solutions except the constant one with value $\lfloor d/2 \rfloor$. These binary constraints were then expressed in a form of explicit representation, as a disjunction of conjunctions of possible assignments, as shown in Figure 3.1.

We generated instances for various choices of the parameters n and d, and solved these using G12 (version 1.4), FznTini, and Minion (version 0.12) — see Table 3.1. As with all of the results presented in this chapter, the times given are elapsed times on a Lenovo 3000 N200 laptop with an Intel Core 2 Duo processor running at 1.66 GHz a 2 GB of RAM. These timings *exclude* the time required to translate the input from MiniZinc to FlatZinc (for input to G12 and FznTini) or from Essence'

---

[3]This middle value was chosen as the constant value so that default value orderings which considered the values for each variable in ascending or descending order did not simply happen to consider the constant value first.

Table 3.1 Average solution times for Minion, G12 and FznTini on constant-closed CSP instances of the form shown in Figure 3.1 which have exactly one solution.

number of CSP variables (n)	number of CSP values (d)	Minion time (s)	G12 time (s)	FznTini time (s)
10	100	1.667	0.117	**0.026**
10	200	13.477	0.330	**0.075**
15	100	41.814	0.207	**0.037**
15	200	482.689	0.571	**0.106**
20	20	2.113	0.044	**0.015**
20	100	> 20 min	0.278	**0.048**
20	200	> 20 min	1.013	**0.138**
30	10	8.571	0.032	**0.016**
50	50	> 20 min	0.367	**0.059**
100	4	> 20 min	0.056	**0.022**
100	10	> 20 min	0.101	**0.033**

to Minion input format. (In the special case of FznTini, times *include* the additional time required to translate from FlatZinc to DIMACS CNF format. Hence, in each case we are measuring the time taken to process the input when presented in a low-level CSP format such as FlatZinc or equivalent.) Average times over five runs with different generated instances are shown, but the variability was found in all cases to be quite small.

It is clear that the most efficient solver for instances of this kind, when presented in this way, is FznTini, which appears to be able to identify the single constant solution extremely rapidly without any specific tuning. The standard constraint solver Minion is significantly less efficient on these instances, which is somewhat surprising since, if the constraints are viewed as binary table constraints, all other values for all of the variables can be eliminated by enforcing arc-consistency, which all of the conventional constraint solvers do by default when propagating constraints. In fact, the translations to FlatZinc and Minion input format do not recognise the constraints as explicit binary constraints, but instead handle the disjunctions by introducing a large number of auxiliary variables, but this is common to all of the solvers tested (including FznTini). When the instances were encoded directly to Minion input format as table constraints, the Minion solver performed as well as G12.

This very simple first set of potential benchmark instances already reveals that there is considerable scope for improving the ability of current CSP-solvers to recognise and exploit structure in the constraints, for example by better recognition and translation of table constraints, or by adapting the value ordering.

3.3 Max-closed constraints

One of the first non-trivial classes of tractable constraint types described in the literature is the class of max-closed constraints introduced in [JC95].

Definition 3.2 ([JC95]) *A constraint (R, S) with relation R of arity r over an ordered domain D is said to be max-closed if for all tuples $(d_1, \ldots, d_r), (d'_1, \ldots, d'_r) \in R$ we have $(max(d_1, d'_1), \ldots, max(d_r, d'_r)) \in R$.*

Some examples of binary max-closed constraints are shown in Figure 3.2. In particular, one useful form of max-closed constraint is an inequality of the form

$$a_1 v_1 + a_2 v_2 + \cdots + a_{r-1} v_{r-1} \geq a_r v_r + c \qquad (3.1)$$

where the v_i are variables, c is a constant, and the a_is are non-negative constants [JC95]. Hence, we constructed a generator which produced random inequalities of this form. An extract from a typical instance specification produced by this generator is shown in Figure 3.3. To generate *solvable* max-closed CSP instances, we selected a random assignment to all of the variables, and then generated random inequalities of the form above, keeping only those that were satisfied by this fixed assignment. This ensured that the system of inequalities had at least one solution. To generate *unsolvable* max-closed CSP instances, we generated the inequalities without imposing this condition; if the resulting set was solvable, another set was generated. Average times over five runs with different instances are shown in Table 3.2.

Fig. 3.2 Examples of binary max-closed constraints from [JC95]. In each rectangle, the circles on the left represent possible values for one variable, and the circles on the right represent possible values for the other variable; both are ordered from bottom to top. Two circles are connected by a line if the constraint allows that combination of values for the two variables.

```
array[1..10] of var 1..5: X;
constraint
97*X[6]  >= 46*X[3] + 16 /\
81*X[5] +88*X[4] +60*X[2] +92*X[7] +28*X[10] >= 43*X[8] + 4 /\
16*X[3] +78*X[10] +61*X[7] +97*X[5] +50*X[8] +30*X[1] >= 19*X[6] + -51;
solve satisfy;
```

Fig. 3.3 A generated max-closed instance specification in MiniZinc with 3 inequalities.

Table 3.2 Average solution times for Minion, G12 and FznTini on max-closed CSP instances of the form shown in Figure 3.3.

number of CSP variables (n)	number of CSP values (d)	number of constraints	Minion time (s)	G12 time (s)	FznTini time (s)
satisfiable instances					
10	100	10	0.353	**0.012**	7.884
10	100	100	0.360	**0.021**	> 20 min
10	200	10	0.354	**0.011**	3.799
20	100	1000	0.490	**0.264**	error
30	200	1000	0.546	**0.457**	error
100	10	10	0.358	**0.021**	1.109
200	100	1000	1.049	**0.067**	error
unsatisfiable instances					
10	100	100	0.058	**0.012**	382.223
20	100	1000	0.082	**0.010**	error
30	200	1000	0.083	**0.071**	error
200	10	1000	0.087	**0.010**	error

The results for these instances are the reverse of those in Section 3.2 — see Table 3.1. Predictably, FznTini performs very poorly on these inequalities, which it has to translate into (large) sets of clauses. (For the larger sets of inequalities we considered it simply gave an "out of memory" error.) Standard CSP-solvers should do well on these instances, because the efficient algorithm for solving max-closed instances is based on achieving arc-consistency, and all standard constraint solvers do this by default. Our results confirm that the standard CSP-solvers do indeed all perform well on these instances without any specific tuning. In particular, they perform much better than FznTini even if the translation time to FlatZinc or Minion input format were to be included in the runtimes.

3.4   0/1/all constraints

Another example of a language-based restriction ensuring tractability involves the 0/1/all constraints introduced and shown to be tractable in [CCJ94].

Definition 3.3 ([CCJ94]) *Let v_1 and v_2 be variables. Let A be a subset of possible values for v_1 and B be a subset of possible values for v_2.*

- *A complete binary constraint is a constraint $R(v_1, v_2)$ of the form $A \times B$.*
- *A permutation constraint is a constraint $R(v_1, v_2)$ which is equal to*
  $\{(d_i, \pi(d_i)) \mid d_i \in A\}$ for some bijection $\pi : A \to B$.

Fig. 3.4 A typical CSP instance with 0/1/all constraints specified in MiniZinc. Note that *complete* constraints are imposed by restricting the domains to some subset, *permutation* constraints are imposed by constraints of the form $X = Y + c \mod d$, and *two-fan* constraints are imposed by constraints of the form $X = d_i \lor Y = d_j$.

```
var {0, 1, 2, 3, 4, 5, 6, 7, 8, 9}: X0;
var {0, 1, 3, 4, 7, 8, 9}: X1;
var {0, 2, 3, 5, 6, 7, 8, 9}: X2;
var {0, 1, 2, 3, 4, 5, 6, 7, 8, 9}: X3;
var {0, 2, 3, 4, 6, 8}: X4;
constraint
((X0 + 7 >= 10) -> (X1 == X0 + 7 - 10)) /\
((X0 + 7 < 10) -> (X1 == X0 + 7)) /\
((X0 == 2) \/ (X2 == 0)) /\
((X1 + 7 >= 10) -> (X3 == X1 + 7 - 10)) /\
((X1 + 7 < 10) -> (X3 == X1 + 7)) /\
((X1 + 9 >= 10) -> (X4 == X1 + 9 - 10)) /\
((X1 + 9 < 10) -> (X4 == X1 + 9)) /\
((X3 == 6) \/ (X2 == 8)) /\
((X3 == 6) \/ (X4 == 6)) ;
solve satisfy;
```

- A two-fan *constraint is a constraint* $R(v_1, v_2)$ *where there exists* $d_i \in A$ *and* $d_j \in B$ *with* $R(v_1, v_2) = (d_i \times B) \cup (A \times d_j)$.

A 0/1/all constraint *is either a complete constraint, a permutation constraint, or a two-fan constraint.*

What is particularly interesting about this form of constraint, for our purposes, is that the efficient algorithm for 0/1/all constraints is based on achieving *path-consistency* [CCJ94], which is not implemented in standard constraint solvers.

To investigate whether instances with 0/1/all constraints are solved efficiently in practice by standard constraint solvers, even without explicitly using path-consistency, we wrote a generator for satisfiable CSP instances with 0/1/all constraints of various kinds on n variables. To ensure satisfiability we first generate a random assignment and then add at random only those 0/1/all constraints that satisfy the initial assignment. An extract from a typical instance specification produced by our generator is shown in Figure 3.4. We generated instances for various choices of the parameters n and d, and solved these using G12, Minion and FznTini. Average timings over five instances are shown in Table 3.3, but the variability is again very small. All the solvers performed very well. We note here that even though on some instances the CSP-solvers performed better than FznTini, the pure solving time of the SAT-solver is shorter than the runtimes shown (since these include the translation time from FlatZinc to SAT).

We also generated unsatisfiable instances with 0/1/all constraints on just a small number of variables, leaving all other variables unconstrained, see Figure 3.5. FznTini and G12 quickly reported "no solutions" (see Table 3.4), but Minion could not solve this problem within 20 min. Interestingly enough, an earlier version of the G12 finite domain solver (0.8.1) was as bad as Minion. Furthermore, the MiniZinc-

Table 3.3 Average solution times for Minion, G12 and FznTini on satisfiable 0/1/all CSP instances of the form shown in Figure 3.4.

number of CSP variables (n)	number of CSP values (d)	Minion time (s)	G12 time (s)	FznTini time (s)
10	100	0.359	**0.018**	0.037
50	100	0.457	**0.276**	0.318
100	10	0.625	0.623	**0.523**
100	50	**0.676**	0.944	0.809
100	100	**0.768**	1.070	0.916

Fig. 3.5 An unsatisfiable CSP instance with 0/1/all constraints on 100 variables with domain size 2 specified in MiniZinc.

```
array[0..99] of var 0..1: X;
constraint
((X[50] == 2) \/ (X[51] == 1)) /\
((X[50] == 1) \/ (X[51] == 2)) /\
((X[50] == 2) \/ (X[51] == 2)) /\
((X[50] == 1) \/ (X[51] == 1)) ;
solve satisfy;
```

Table 3.4 Average solution times for Minion, FznTini and two versions of G12 on unsatisfiable 0/1/all CSP instances of the form shown in Figure 3.5.

number of CSP variables (n)	number of CSP values (d)	Minion time (s)	G12 (v0.8.1) time (s)	G12 (v1.4) time (s)	FznTini time (s)
100	2	> 20 min	> 20 min	**0.012**	0.058

to-FlatZinc translator distributed with that version of G12 produced a much larger FlatZinc instance than the one available with the G12 suite version 1.4. This could be the reason why the older version of G12 performed so badly, however, version 1.4 of the finite domain solver performed well even on the old FlatZinc instance.

The problem with this simple unsatisfiable 0/1/all instance shown in Figure 3.5 seems to be the fixed default variable ordering: Minion (and G12 version 0.8.1) tries every possible combination of values for the first 49 unconstrained variables before it reports that the problem does not have a solution. It does not focus the search on the few variables that are restricted; having no constraint between two variables is treated in the same way as having a complete constraint. Once the unsatisfiable instances were added to the satisfiable ones (used for Table 3.3), the performance of Minion (and G12 version 0.8.1) was as good as before.

These results suggest that standard CSP-solvers can handle random collections of 0/1/all constraints very effectively, even without specialised algorithms. However, they appear to be poor at focusing search on more highly constrained regions, which is thought to be one of the strengths of the current generation of SAT-solvers. This suggests an obvious target for improvement in adapting the variable ordering to the specific features of the input instance.

3.5 Connected-row-convex constraints

Connected-row-convex constraints were first defined in [DBvH99] using a standard matrix representation of binary relations.

Definition 3.4 ([DBvH99]) *Let the domain D be the ordered set $\{d_1, d_2, \cdots, d_m\}$, where $d_1 < d_2 < \cdots < d_m$. A binary relation R over D can be represented by an $m \times m$ 0–1 matrix M, by setting $M_{ij} = 1$ if the relation contains the pair (d_i, d_j) and $M_{ij} = 0$ otherwise. A relation is said to be* connected-row-convex *if the pattern of 1's in the matrix representation (after removing rows and columns containing only 0's) is connected along each row, along each column, and forms a connected 2-dimensional region (where some of the connections may be diagonal).*

Any binary constraint whose constraint relation is connected-row-convex will be called a connected-row-convex constraint; some examples are illustrated in Figure 3.6. It is convenient to also define all unary constraints to be connected-row-convex, as they may be combined with binary connected-row-convex constraints to obtain a larger tractable class of problems [CJJK00]. An example of a constraint that is not connected-row-convex is shown in Figure 3.7. The 0 marked in bold in the middle makes the pattern of 1s not connected along the row (and column) it is in.

The so-called *staircase constraints* [DBvH99] are also connected-row-convex.

Definition 3.5 *[DBvH99] Let $\preceq$ and $\succeq$ be total orderings on D_i and D_j, respectively. A (binary) constraint C_{ij} is $(\preceq, \succeq)$-monotone if*

- $\forall v, v' \in D_i, \forall w \in D_j$: *if $C_{ij}(v, w)$ and $v' \preceq v$ then $C_{ij}(v', w)$,*
- $\forall v \in D_i, \forall w, w' \in D_j$: *if $C_{ij}(v, w)$ and $w' \succeq w$ then $C_{ij}(v, w')$.*

A constraint is staircase *if it is (α, β)-monotone with $\alpha, \beta \in \{\leq, \geq\}$.*

$$
\begin{pmatrix}
0 & 0 & 0 & 0 & 0 & 1 & 0 & 0 & 0 & 0 \\
0 & 0 & 0 & 1 & 1 & 1 & 1 & 0 & 0 & 0 \\
0 & 0 & 0 & 1 & 1 & 1 & 1 & 0 & 1 & 0 \\
0 & 1 & 1 & 1 & 1 & 1 & 1 & 0 & 1 & 0 \\
1 & 1 & 1 & 1 & 1 & 1 & 1 & 0 & 1 & 1 \\
0 & 1 & 1 & 1 & 1 & 1 & 1 & 0 & 1 & 0 \\
0 & 0 & 1 & 1 & 1 & 1 & 1 & 0 & 1 & 0 \\
0 & 0 & 1 & 1 & 1 & 1 & 1 & 0 & 1 & 0 \\
0 & 0 & 0 & 1 & 1 & 0 & 0 & 0 & 0 & 0 \\
0 & 0 & 0 & 0 & 1 & 0 & 0 & 0 & 0 & 0
\end{pmatrix}
\begin{pmatrix}
1 & 1 & 0 & 0 & 0 & 0 & 0 & 0 & 0 & 0 \\
1 & 1 & 0 & 0 & 0 & 0 & 0 & 0 & 0 & 0 \\
0 & 0 & 1 & 1 & 1 & 0 & 0 & 0 & 0 & 0 \\
0 & 0 & 1 & 1 & 1 & 0 & 0 & 0 & 0 & 0 \\
0 & 0 & 1 & 1 & 1 & 0 & 0 & 0 & 0 & 0 \\
0 & 0 & 1 & 1 & 1 & 0 & 0 & 0 & 0 & 0 \\
0 & 0 & 0 & 0 & 0 & 1 & 1 & 1 & 1 & 1 \\
0 & 0 & 0 & 0 & 0 & 1 & 1 & 1 & 1 & 1 \\
0 & 0 & 0 & 0 & 0 & 1 & 1 & 1 & 0 & 0 \\
0 & 0 & 0 & 0 & 0 & 1 & 1 & 1 & 0 & 0
\end{pmatrix}
\begin{pmatrix}
0 & 0 & 0 & 0 & 0 & 0 & 0 & 1 & 0 & 0 \\
0 & 0 & 0 & 0 & 0 & 0 & 1 & 1 & 0 & 0 \\
0 & 0 & 0 & 0 & 0 & 0 & 1 & 1 & 0 & 0 \\
0 & 0 & 0 & 0 & 0 & 0 & 1 & 1 & 1 & 1 \\
0 & 0 & 0 & 0 & 0 & 0 & 1 & 1 & 1 & 0 \\
0 & 0 & 0 & 0 & 1 & 1 & 0 & 0 & 0 & 0 \\
0 & 0 & 0 & 0 & 1 & 0 & 0 & 0 & 0 & 0 \\
1 & 1 & 1 & 1 & 0 & 0 & 0 & 0 & 0 & 0 \\
0 & 1 & 1 & 1 & 0 & 0 & 0 & 0 & 0 & 0 \\
0 & 0 & 1 & 1 & 0 & 0 & 0 & 0 & 0 & 0
\end{pmatrix}
$$

Fig. 3.6 Examples of connected-row-convex relations from [CJJK00].

Fig. 3.7 An example of a
relation that is not
connected-row-convex. Note
that if the 0 marked in bold
were changed to 1, then this
relation would be
connected-row-convex.

$$
\begin{pmatrix}
0 & 0 & 0 & 0 & 0 & 1 & 0 & 0 & 0 & 0 \\
0 & 0 & 0 & 0 & 1 & 1 & 1 & 0 & 0 & 0 \\
0 & 0 & 0 & 1 & 1 & 1 & 1 & 0 & 1 & 0 \\
0 & 1 & 1 & 1 & 1 & 1 & 1 & 0 & 1 & 0 \\
1 & 1 & 1 & 1 & \mathbf{0} & 1 & 1 & 0 & 1 & 1 \\
0 & 1 & 1 & 1 & 1 & 1 & 1 & 0 & 1 & 0 \\
0 & 0 & 1 & 1 & 1 & 1 & 1 & 0 & 1 & 0 \\
0 & 0 & 1 & 1 & 1 & 1 & 1 & 0 & 1 & 0 \\
0 & 0 & 0 & 1 & 1 & 0 & 0 & 0 & 0 & 0 \\
0 & 0 & 0 & 0 & 1 & 0 & 0 & 0 & 0 & 0
\end{pmatrix}
$$

Fig. 3.8 A generated
connected-row-convex
instance specification in
Essence' with 3 inequalities
for $n = 4$ and $d = 5$.

```
language ESSENCE' 1.b.a
letting D be domain int(1..4)
find X : matrix indexed by [D] of int(1..5)
such that
46*X[1] +7*X[4] >= -79 ,
1*X[1] +70*X[3] <= 6 ,
27*X[2] +4*X[3] <= 78
```

Staircase constraints include, among others, inequalities of the form:

$$av_1 + bv_2 \geq c$$
$$av_1 + bv_2 \leq c$$

where a, b and c are constants and v_is are variables.

We constructed a generator which produced random inequalities of this form on n variables with domain size d. An extract from a typical instance specification produced by this generator is shown in Figure 3.8. To generate *solvable* connected-row-convex CSP instances, we selected a random assignment to all of the variables, and then generated random inequalities of the form above, keeping only those that were satisfied by this fixed assignment. This ensured that the system of inequalities had at least one solution. Average times over five runs with different instances are shown in Table 3.5.

On this simple set of instances all solvers performed very well, although Minion was noticeably slightly slower. It is worth mentioning that most of these instances were essentially solved at the translation stage. That is, both G12's MiniZinc-to-FlatZinc translator as well as Tailor produced significantly smaller instances with just a few inequalities satisfying the original instances (see Figure 3.9), or some trivially unsatisfiable constraints in the unsatisfiable cases. Again pure solving time of FznTini was sightly better than the runtimes shown, since these include the translation time from FlatZinc to SAT.

Table 3.5 Average solution times for Minion, G12 and FznTini on connected-row-convex CSP instances of the form shown in Figure 3.8.

number of CSP variables (n)	number of CSP values (d)	number of constraints	Minion time (s)	G12 time (s)	FznTini time (s)
satisfiable instances					
10	100	10	0.355	0.011	0.011
10	100	100	0.358	0.010	0.012
10	200	10	0.357	0.011	0.011
20	100	1000	0.358	0.016	0.014
30	200	1000	0.359	0.015	0.016
100	10	10	0.358	0.020	0.022
200	100	1000	0.363	0.065	0.065
unsatisfiable instances					
10	100	100	0.058	0.010	0.010
20	100	1000	0.062	0.011	0.011
30	200	1000	0.063	0.010	0.011
200	10	1000	0.065	0.010	0.011

Fig. 3.9 Connected-row-convex instance in Minion input format. The instance was produced by Tailor, which was run on an Essence' instance containing originally 100 constraints.

```
MINION 3
**VARIABLES**
DISCRETE X[10] {1..100}
**SEARCH**
PRINT [X]
VARORDER [X]
**CONSTRAINTS**
weightedsumgeq([17,31], [X[9],X[4]], 65)
weightedsumgeq([7,60], [X[8],X[2]], 88)
weightedsumgeq([22,45], [X[8],X[4]], 67)
weightedsumgeq([4,11], [X[8],X[6]], 63)
weightedsumgeq([10,34], [X[1],X[9]], 78)
weightedsumgeq([22,42], [X[6],X[8]], 81)
**EOF**
```

3.6 Bounded-width structures

For our final example, we consider classes of CSP instances which are tractable because of the way that the constraint scopes are chosen. In other words, we consider structural restrictions, that is restrictions on the hypergraph (see Definition 2.8) of a given CSP instance.

If we impose certain conditions on the kinds of structure we allow an instance to have, then this can be sufficient to ensure tractability for all possible CSP

MiniZinc

```
array[1..7] of var 0..2: X1;
array[1..7] of var 0..2: X2;
array[1..7] of var 0..2: X3;
constraint
forall(i in 1..6)(
X1[i]+X2[i]+X3[i]
   <
X1[i+1]+X2[i+1]+X3[i+1]);
solve satisfy;
```

Essence'

```
language ESSENCE' 1.b.a
letting D be domain int(1..7)
letting E be domain int(1..6)
find X1 : matrix indexed by [D]
  of int(0..2)
find X2 : matrix indexed by [D]
  of int(0..2)
find X3 : matrix indexed by [D]
  of int(0..2)
such that
forall i : E. (
X1[i]+X2[i]+X3[i]
   <
X1[i+1]+X2[i+1]+X3[i+1])
```

Fig. 3.10 Generated specification in MiniZinc and Essence' for a CSP instance with bounded-width structure, where $w = 3$ and $d = 3$.

instances with structures satisfying those conditions, regardless of the type of constraints [Gro06]. In particular, one very simple condition which is sufficient to ensure tractability is to require the structure to have a *tree-decomposition* [DP87, KV00a, CR97], with some fixed bound on the maximum number of vertices in any node of the tree. Such structures are said to have *bounded-width*.

However, the efficient algorithm for CSP instances with bounded-width structures is based on choosing an appropriate variable ordering, and imposing a level of consistency proportional to the width [DKV02, DP89, Fre90]. None of the standard CSP-solvers incorporate this algorithm, so it is not at all evident whether they can solve bounded-width instances efficiently.

To investigate this question we wrote a generator for a family of specific CSP instances with a very simple bounded-width structure.

The instances we generate are specified by two parameters, w and d. They have $[(d-1)w+1]*w$ variables arranged in groups of size w, each with domain $\{0, \ldots, d-1\}$. We impose a constraint of arity $2w$ on each pair of successive groups, requiring that the sum of the values assigned to the first of these two groups should be smaller than the sum of the values assigned to the second. This ensures that a solution exists and satisfies the following conditions: the difference between the sum of values assigned to each successive group is 1, and the sum of the values assigned to the last group is zero. An extract from a typical instance specification produced by our generator is shown in Figure 3.10.

When $w = 1$, the generated instances have a single line of binary constraints, so they have a tree structure, and can be efficiently solved using arc-consistency. For this special case, all of the solvers are able to solve the instances very quickly (see the first row of Table 3.6).

For larger values of w, the generated instances have larger width, but still bounded by $2w - 1$, because their structure has a simple tree-decomposition as a

Table 3.6 Average solution times for Minion, G12 and FznTini on satisfiable bounded-width CSP instances of the form shown in Figure 3.10.

group size (w)	number of CSP values (d)	number of CSP variables (n)	Minion time (s)	G12 time (s)	FznTini time (s)
1	100	100	0.355	**0.015**	0.263
2	6	22	0.354	0.088	**0.039**
2	7	26	0.354	23.470	**0.088**
2	8	30	0.354	667.995	**0.052**
2	9	34	0.354	414.904	**0.312**
2	10	38	0.353	> 20 min	**0.264**
3	3	21	0.354	**0.014**	0.018
3	4	30	0.402	2.480	**0.085**
3	5	39	11.041	> 20 min	**0.138**
3	6	48	> 20 min	> 20 min	**1.449**

Table 3.7 Average solution times for Minion, G12 and FznTini on satisfiable bounded-width CSP instances of the form shown in Figure 3.10 with inequalities reversed.

group size (w)	number of CSP values (d)	number of CSP variables (n)	Minion time (s)	G12 time (s)	FznTini time (s)
1	100	100	0.360	**0.015**	0.193
2	6	22	0.928	**0.012**	0.045
2	7	26	27.569	**0.011**	0.078
2	8	30	> 20 min	**0.012**	0.169
2	9	34	> 20 min	**0.013**	0.325
2	10	38	> 20 min	**0.012**	0.237
3	3	21	0.420	**0.012**	0.024
3	4	30	764.065	**0.019**	0.056
3	5	39	> 20 min	0.430	**0.038**
3	6	48	> 20 min	6.145	**0.668**

path of nodes, with each node corresponding to a single constraint scope. In this case, although the problem is still tractable according to Definition 3.1, it cannot be solved efficiently using standard propagation algorithms. In fact, the runtime of G12 grows rapidly with problem size, as shown in Table 3.6.

The runtimes for the Minion solver do not increase so fast for these specific instances, but if we reverse the inequalities, then they do increase in the same way (see Table 3.7), although in this case G12 performs much better. Somewhat surprisingly, FznTini seems to be able to solve all of these instances fairly efficiently, even though they contain arithmetic inequalities which have to be translated into fairly large sets of clauses.

It is clear from these results that G12 and Minion do not take advantage of the simple structure of the instance they are attempting to solve. Hence an important opportunity to improve the performance of CSP-solvers would be in finding an efficient way of taking advantage of instance structure by adapting the variable ordering or other aspects of the search process to the particular instance. Moreover, as the ordering can be set in the input file, the question arises as to whether those adjustments could be automatically identified by the translators as part of the pre-processing.

3.7 Summary

We believe that the results presented in this chapter have established that the various ideas about different forms of tractable constraint satisfaction instances presented in the theoretical literature can provide a fruitful source of inspiration for the design of challenging benchmark instances.

The initial applications of these ideas, presented in the previous sections, have already identified significant differences between different solvers in their ability to exploit important features of the problem instances they are given.

There are a number of technical difficulties to overcome in developing useful benchmark instances. First of all, unlike SAT-solvers, there is no standard input language for CSP-solvers. Some progress has been made in proposing standard specification languages, and in providing automatic translation between different input languages, but these are currently far from complete. We have seen in Section 3.2 that the translation from MiniZinc to FlatZinc, or from Essence' to Minion, can sometimes obscure the nature of an essentially simple problem, and hence badly affect the efficiency of the solution. We suggest that a better awareness of the factors of a problem specification that can ensure tractability could lead to better translation software, which ensures that such features are preserved. In particular, identifying tractable parts of an instance specification could lead to pre-processing tools that would automatically annotate such features in a way that could be exploited by a solver. This might be a simple matter of identifying useful value or variable orderings, or it might mean packaging some parts of the instance into (tractable) global constraints that can then use dedicated propagation algorithms to take advantage of their structure.

SAT-solvers avoid many of the difficulties of translating between different input languages by adopting a single standard format for the input: all constraints must be expressed as clauses in CNF. However, the cost of this standardisation is a loss of expressive power. We have seen in Section 3.3 that translating simple forms of constraints such as linear inequalities into CNF may be very inefficient, and may lose the important features of the constraints which guarantee tractability.

Even when they have been successfully captured in an appropriate specification language, and input to a constraint solver, it can be the case that theoretically tractable instances may still be solved very inefficiently in practice. We have seen in Sections 3.4, and especially in Section 3.6, that when the tractability is due to a property that requires a higher level of consistency than arc-consistency to exploit, instances may be very challenging for standard solvers. It may be that this gap between theoretical notions of tractability, as expressed in Definition 3.1, and efficient solvability in practice, can suggest additional refinements that can usefully be added to the constraint-solving armoury (for example, some notion of adaptive consistency that invokes higher-levels of consistency when they can be easily shown to be effective). The dramatic progress in SAT-solving technology that has resulted from the exploitation of heuristics, such as clause learning and random restarts, that serve to focus the search more effectively, is an encouraging precedent. Finding effective automatic ways to improve the variable orderings and value orderings used by a solver according to specific relevant features of the input instance seems a promising first step which has not been sufficiently pursued. For example, the connection between having a bounded-width structure and the existence of a variable ordering with certain favourable properties (such as bounded *induced width*) is well known [Fre90, DP89, DKV02] but does not seem to have been explored in any of the solvers or translation tools used in this study.

Furthermore, this chapter has revealed that SAT-based constraint solvers are sometimes much more efficient than conventional solvers on certain families of CSP instances (see Section 3.2 and 3.6). Moreover, we previously conducted some experiments on the same set of instances used in this chapter but with versions of the solvers from 2009. By comparing these results with the ones obtained in this chapter we conclude that the G12 finite domain solver (version 1.4) performs much better than its older version on all sets of instances, even though it still struggles in the case of instances with bounded-width structure[4].

In order to explore the efficient behaviour of SAT-based constraint solvers we first explain how a CSP instance can be translated into SAT in the next chapter. Then we provide theoretical reasons why SAT-solvers are so efficient on certain families of CSP instances and compare well-known SAT and constraint solvers experimentally (see Chapters 5 and 6).

---

[4]We also tested the performance of the Gecode solver. The latest version of the solver achieved comparable results with G12. The version from 2009 performed as badly as the other standard constraint solvers at that time.

Chapter 4
SAT encodings

I don't think necessity is the mother of invention. Invention, in my opinion, arises directly from idleness, possibly also from laziness — to save oneself trouble.

Agatha Christie

One of the most surprising discoveries in constraint-solving in the last decade has been the remarkable performance of SAT-solvers on many constraint satisfaction problems. Even though a lot of information about the original CSP instance is usually lost at the translation stage and a large set of propositional clauses is produced, SAT-solvers sometimes outperform conventional CSP-solvers on such instances (see Chapter 3). Furthermore, SAT-solvers often perform well even on instances that were encoded using the most naive encoding (called the direct encoding, see below).

In an attempt to compare various solving techniques used for CSP and SAT several different ways of encoding a CSP instance as a propositional formula have been proposed. These have successfully been used in SAT-based constraint solvers. Some encodings that have been developed are very problem-specific. However, this book deals with just the most commonly used ones that encode the general CSP. These are categorised here based on the information each Boolean variable carries about variables in the original CSP.

4.1 Sparse encodings

Probably the first encoding introduced was the *direct encoding*. In this encoding, for every variable-value pair a separate Boolean variable is introduced. We will call such variables *assignment variables* since if, for instance, variable v is assigned value a, then the corresponding Boolean variable x_{va} is set to *True*. On the other hand if v is assigned the value b and $a \neq b$, then x_{va} is set to *False*. From now on we will refer to the class of encodings that contain only assignment variables as *sparse encodings* (this term was introduced in [Hoo99]). We will say that a partial assignment f *falsifies* a clause C if C consists entirely of literals of the form $\neg x_{vf(v)}$,

© Springer International Publishing Switzerland 2015
J. Petke, *Bridging Constraint Satisfaction and Boolean Satisfiability*,
Artificial Intelligence: Foundations, Theory, and Algorithms,
DOI 10.1007/978-3-319-21810-6_4

for the set of variables on which f is defined. Otherwise, we will say that a partial assignment f *satisfies* a clause C.

Example 4.1 *Let P be a CSP instance such that $V = \{u, v, w\}$, $D_u = D_v = \{0, 1\}$, $D_w = \{0, 1, 2\}$ and C contains a single ternary constraint with scope (u, v, w) specifying that $u \leq v < w$. A sparse encoding of P will introduce seven Boolean variables:*

$$x_{u0}, \ x_{u1}, \ x_{v0}, \ x_{v1}, \ x_{w0}, \ x_{w1}, \ x_{w2}$$

Sparse encodings usually contain certain clauses known as *at-least-one* and *at-most-one* clauses, to ensure that each variable v is assigned a value, say i, and that no other value, $j \neq i$, is assigned to v. The at-least-one clauses are of the form $\bigvee_{i \in D_v} x_{vi}$ for each variable v. The at-most-one clauses can be represented as a set of binary clauses $\neg x_{vi} \vee \neg x_{vj}$ for all $i, j \in D_v$ with $i \neq j$.

Example 4.2 *In the case of the CSP instance from Example 4.1 the at-least-one clauses are:*

$$x_{u0} \vee x_{u1}, \ x_{v0} \vee x_{v1}, \ x_{w0} \vee x_{w1} \vee x_{w2}$$

The at-most-one clauses are:

$$\neg x_{u0} \vee \neg x_{u1}, \ \neg x_{v0} \vee \neg x_{v1}, \ \neg x_{w0} \vee \neg x_{w1}, \ \neg x_{w0} \vee \neg x_{w2}, \ \neg x_{w1} \vee \neg x_{w2}$$

The various different sparse encodings differ in the way they encode the constraints of a CSP instance. Two methods are most commonly used. The first one encodes the *disallowed* variable assignments — the so-called *conflicts* or *nogoods*. The *direct encoding* [Pre09], for instance, generates a clause $\bigvee_{v \in S} \neg x_{vf(v)}$ for each partial assignment f that does *not* satisfy the constraint $(R, S) \in C$.

Example 4.3 *Using the direct encoding, the ternary constraint from Example 4.1 would be encoded by the following clauses:*

$$\neg x_{u0} \vee \neg x_{v0} \vee \neg x_{w0}$$
$$\neg x_{u0} \vee \neg x_{v1} \vee \neg x_{w0}$$
$$\neg x_{u0} \vee \neg x_{v1} \vee \neg x_{w1}$$
$$\neg x_{u1} \vee \neg x_{v0} \vee \neg x_{w0}$$
$$\neg x_{u1} \vee \neg x_{v0} \vee \neg x_{w1}$$
$$\neg x_{u1} \vee \neg x_{v0} \vee \neg x_{w2}$$
$$\neg x_{u1} \vee \neg x_{v1} \vee \neg x_{w0}$$
$$\neg x_{u1} \vee \neg x_{v1} \vee \neg x_{w1}$$

Another way of translating constraints into clauses is to encode the *allowed* variable assignments — the so-called *supports*. This has been used as the basis for an encoding of binary CSP instances, known as the *support encoding* [Gen02], defined as follows. For each pair of variables v, w in the scope of some constraint, and each value $i \in D_v$, the support encoding will contain the clause $\neg x_{vi} \vee \bigvee_{j \in A} x_{wj}$, where $A \subseteq D_w$ is the set of values for the variable w which are compatible with the assignment $v = i$, according to the constraint.

Note that the support encoding is defined for binary CSP instances only. However, some non-binary constraints can be decomposed into binary ones without introducing any new variables.

Example 4.4 *The ternary constraint from Example 4.1 can be decomposed into two binary constraints specifying that $u \leq v$ and $v < w$. Using the support encoding, these binary constraints would then be represented by the following clauses:*

$$\neg x_{u0} \vee x_{v0} \vee x_{v1}$$
$$\neg x_{u1} \vee x_{v1}$$
$$\neg x_{v0} \vee x_{u0}, \quad \neg x_{v0} \vee x_{w1} \vee x_{w2}$$
$$\neg x_{v1} \vee x_{u0} \vee x_{u1}, \quad \neg x_{v1} \vee x_{w2}$$
$$\neg x_{w0}$$
$$\neg x_{w1} \vee x_{v0}$$
$$\neg x_{w2} \vee x_{v0} \vee x_{v1}$$

Other sparse encodings one can find in the literature include the *multivalued direct encoding* [SLM92] and the *minimal support encoding* [ACLM08a]. The first encoding looks exactly the same as the direct encoding except that the at-most-one clauses are omitted. Even though such an encoding allows for multiple simultanous assignments to the same CSP variable, a concrete solution can be recovered by selecting any one of the assignments for each CSP variable. The minimal support encoding is similar to the support encoding except that, for every constraint with scope v, w, we only add either the support clauses for all the domain values of the CSP variable v or the support clauses for all the domain values of the CSP variable w.

Example 4.5 *Only the following constraint clauses will occur in the minimal support encoding of the Example 4.1:*

$$\neg x_{u0} \vee x_{v0} \vee x_{v1}$$
$$\neg x_{u1} \vee x_{v1}$$
$$\neg x_{v0} \vee x_{w1} \vee x_{w2}$$
$$\neg x_{v1} \vee x_{w2}$$

Unlike in the case of the support encoding [Gen02], unit propagation on the minimal support encoding does not enforce arc-consistency [ACLM08b].

A sparse encoding of a CSP instance can be easily recognised by looking at the structure of the Boolean encoding.

Lemma 4.6 *Let Φ be a Boolean propositional formula in conjunctive normal form. Let $\Gamma \subset \Phi$ be a set of disjoint purely positive clauses. If every Boolean variable that belongs to Φ also belongs to Γ and for each clause $\gamma \in \Gamma$, Φ allows only one of the literals in γ to be satisfied, then Φ is a sparse encoding of some CSP problem P.*

Proof Let Φ and Γ be defined as above. Let $\gamma = \bigvee_i x_{vi}$ be a clause in Γ. Then at least one of the x_{vi}s must be assigned the value *True*. As Φ disallows $x_{vi} \wedge x_{vj}$ for all $i \neq j$, at most one of the x_{vi}s can be assigned *True*. Hence, γ can be viewed as a CSP variable with domain size $|\gamma|$. Let γ represent a CSP variable v_γ. Let $V = \{v_\gamma \mid \gamma \in \Gamma\}$ and $D = \{D_{v_\gamma} = \{1, \cdots, |\gamma|\} \mid \gamma \in \Gamma\}$. As Γ contains all variables that occur in Φ, each clause $\gamma' \notin \Gamma$ can be viewed as a constraint. Note that each literal in γ' represents either a variable assignment, say $v_\gamma = i$, or is a negation of some variable assignment, $v_\gamma \neq i$. Let $C = \{\gamma' \mid \gamma' \in \Phi \wedge \gamma' \notin \Gamma\}$. Then Φ is a sparse encoding of the CSP problem $P = (V, D, C)$. $\square$

Note that we have assumed in Lemma 4.6 that a sparse encoding must contain the appropriate at-least-one clauses. In fact, this does not necessarily need to be true.

Lemma 4.7 *Let Φ be a Boolean propositional formula in conjunctive normal form and let X be the set of variables of Φ. Divide X into disjoint subsets X_i. If Φ forces exactly one of $x \in X_i$ to be satisfied for each X_i, then Φ is a sparse encoding of some CSP P.*

Proof Let $\Phi' = \Phi \wedge \bigwedge_{X_i \in X}(\bigvee_{x \in X_i} x)$. Then Φ' fulfills the conditions in Lemma 4.6 and the proof follows. $\square$

4.2   The log encoding

The *log encoding* [Wal00] introduces a Boolean variable for each *bit* in the value of a CSP variable. For instance, a variable v with domain $\{0, 1, 2, 3\}$ will be encoded using two Boolean variables, x_{v0} and x_{v1}. In this case the Boolean assignment ($x_{v0} =$ *False*, $x_{v1} =$ *True*) corresponds to the CSP assignment $v = 2$. The at-least-one and at-most-one clauses are not needed in the log encoding, since every bit pattern represents a potential solution. However, unary constraints can be imposed to rule out certain bit patterns, and hence restrict the values of a variable to some subset of the domain. Once again, clauses are added to represent the constraints, by ruling out any assignment that violates a constraint. The constraints are represented as conflicts.

Example 4.8 *Assume we are encoding the constraint $v + w \geq 2$ and the domain for v and w is $\{0, 1, 2, 3\}$. There are three tuples that violate the inequality, $(0, 0)$, $(0, 1)$ and $(1, 0)$. Hence, the following clauses will be generated:*

$$x_{v0} \vee x_{v1} \vee x_{w0} \vee x_{w1}$$
$$x_{v0} \vee x_{v1} \vee \neg x_{w0} \vee x_{w1}$$
$$\neg x_{v0} \vee x_{v1} \vee x_{w0} \vee x_{w1}$$

4.3   Regular and interval-based encodings

Sparse encodings are usually inefficient in practice, since they often produce very large sets of clauses.

Example 4.9 *Suppose the domains of variables v and w in Example 4.1 are much larger, say $D_v = D_w = \{0, 1000\}$. Then the support encoding would introduce the following clauses to encode the constraint $v < w$:*

$$\neg x_{v0} \vee x_{w1} \vee x_{w2} \cdots \vee x_{w1000}$$
$$\neg x_{v1} \vee x_{w2} \vee x_{w3} \cdots \vee x_{w1000}$$
$$\cdots$$
$$\neg x_{v999} \vee x_{w1000}$$
$$\neg x_{v1000}$$

In the case above it might be more efficient to be able to represent the intervals $i \ldots 1000$ for $1 \le i \le 999$ more succinctly. That is why another way of encoding CSP domains was proposed which introduces Boolean variables representing *comparisons*. Such variables are called *ladder variables* [GN04] or *regular variables* [AM04]. We will use the latter terminology.

A regular variable $x_{vi}^{\ge}$ is a Boolean variable that is set to the value *True* if and only if variable v is assigned a value that is greater than or equal to value i. A *regular encoding* can be based on any sparse encoding. The domains are encoded using regular variables. The constraints are encoded in the same way as in a sparse encoding on which it is based.

Example 4.10 *The regular minimal support encoding of Example 4.1 is as follows.*

The domain clauses:

$$x_{u0} \leftrightarrow \neg x_{u1}^{\ge} \qquad\qquad x_{u1}^{\ge} \rightarrow x_{u0}^{\ge}$$
$$x_{v0} \leftrightarrow \neg x_{v1}^{\ge} \qquad\qquad x_{v1}^{\ge} \rightarrow x_{v0}^{\ge}$$
$$x_{w0} \leftrightarrow \neg x_{w1}^{\ge} \qquad\qquad x_{w1}^{\ge} \rightarrow x_{w0}^{\ge}$$
$$x_{w1} \leftrightarrow x_{w1}^{\ge} \wedge \neg x_{w2}^{\ge} \qquad x_{w2}^{\ge} \rightarrow x_{w1}^{\ge}$$
$$x_{w2} \leftrightarrow x_{w2}^{\ge}$$

The constraint clauses:

$$\neg x_{u0} \vee x_{v0} \vee x_{v1}$$
$$\neg x_{u1} \vee x_{v1}$$
$$\neg x_{v0} \vee x_{w1} \vee x_{w2}$$
$$\neg x_{v1} \vee x_{w2}$$

Note that the last four domain clauses encode the condition that if a variable is greater than or equal to some value i, then it is also greater than or equal to any value smaller than i. These are the so-called *ladder clauses*, whereas the first five domain clauses are usually called the *channelling clauses* [GN04].

Example 4.11 *In a regular encoding the domain clauses representing a CSP variable v with domain $\{1, \cdots , m\}$ can be split into the following two sets of clauses encoding the at-least-one and at-most-one conditions [ACLM10]:*

$$at\text{-}least\text{-}one\ constraint:$$

$$x_{v1} \leftarrow \neg x_{v2}^{\geq}$$
$$x_{vi} \leftarrow x_{vi}^{\geq} \wedge \neg x_{v(i+1)}^{\geq} \quad for\ all\ 2 \leq i \leq m-1$$
$$x_{vm} \leftarrow x_{vm}^{\geq}$$

$$at\text{-}most\text{-}one\ constraint:$$

$$x_{v1} \rightarrow \neg x_{v2}^{\geq}$$
$$x_{vi} \rightarrow x_{vi}^{\geq} \wedge \neg x_{v(i+1)}^{\geq} \quad for\ all\ 2 \leq i \leq m-1$$
$$x_{vm} \rightarrow x_{vm}^{\geq}$$
$$x_{v(i+1)}^{\geq} \rightarrow x_{vi}^{\geq} \quad for\ all\ 1 \leq i \leq m-1$$

Another possibility of encoding a CSP instance into SAT is to use regular variables only. The simplest example are the *full regular encodings* [ACLM09]. In this case all variables in a sparse encoding are converted into regular ones. The domain clauses need only to contain the ladder clauses.

Example 4.12 *The full regular minimal support encoding of our running example is as follows.*

$$The\ domain\ clauses:$$

$$x_{u1}^{\geq} \rightarrow x_{u0}^{\geq}$$
$$x_{v1}^{\geq} \rightarrow x_{v0}^{\geq}$$
$$x_{w1}^{\geq} \rightarrow x_{w0}^{\geq}$$
$$x_{w2}^{\geq} \rightarrow x_{w1}^{\geq}$$

$$The\ constraint\ clauses:$$

$$\neg x_{u0}^{\geq} \vee x_{v0}^{\geq} \vee x_{v1}^{\geq}, \ \neg x_{u0}^{\geq} \vee x_{v0}^{\geq} \vee \neg x_{v0}^{\geq}$$
$$\neg x_{u1}^{\geq} \vee x_{u0}^{\geq} \vee x_{v1}^{\geq}, \ \neg x_{u1}^{\geq} \vee x_{u0}^{\geq} \vee \neg x_{v0}^{\geq}$$
$$\neg x_{v0}^{\geq} \vee x_{w1}^{\geq} \vee x_{w2}^{\geq}, \ \neg x_{v0}^{\geq} \vee x_{w1}^{\geq} \vee \neg x_{w1}^{\geq}, \ \neg x_{v0}^{\geq} \vee \neg x_{w0}^{\geq} \vee x_{w2}^{\geq}, \ \neg x_{v0}^{\geq} \vee \neg x_{w0}^{\geq} \vee \neg x_{w1}^{\geq}$$
$$\neg x_{v1}^{\geq} \vee x_{v0}^{\geq} \vee x_{w2}^{\geq}, \ \neg x_{v1}^{\geq} \vee x_{v0}^{\geq} \vee \neg x_{w1}^{\geq}$$

Another example of a SAT encoding that contains regular variables only is the *order encoding* [TTKB09]. In this encoding the domain clauses contain the appropriate ladder clauses and the constraints are encoded using disallowed regions (for more details see Section 6.3).

Other encodings that use regular variables include the *half-regular encodings* [AM04] and the *interval-based regular encodings* [ACLM12]. The latter type of encoding is essentially a translation of a sparse encoding into a full regular one by using intervals. It is worth mentioning that this method helps avoid exponential blowup at the translation stage [ACLM10].

In order to reduce the size of a SAT encoding of a CSP instance, *interval-based encodings* have also been introduced. In those encodings each Boolean variable represents a domain interval, that is $x^{[]}_{vij}$, when set to *True*, means that the value for variable v is in the interval $[i,j]$. Such interval-based encodings have been used to encode the alldifferent and cardinality constraints [BKN$^+$09, FG10]. Note that each interval variable $x^{[]}_{vij}$ can be represented by a conjunction of two regular variables, that is $x^{\geq}_{vi} \wedge \neg x^{\geq}_{v(j+1)}$.

4.4 Other encodings

In the SAT encodings described thus far each Boolean variable represents some restriction on the domain of *one* CSP variable it represents. One can, however, introduce variables representing a SAT formula in the assignment variables. Those auxiliary variables frequently help produce more compact and efficient encodings. However, such encodings are usually not generalisable as they are frequently defined for a specific (global) constraint. An example is the *at-most-k* constraint, which imposes the restriction that at most k Boolean variables can be assigned the value *True*. Among SAT encodings proposed for this constraint is the *sequential counter encoding* [Sin05] and the *commander encoding* [FG10]. Various encodings for the pigeonhole problem are also discussed in Chapter 7.

Furthermore, a wide range of constraints can be represented as linear constraints over Boolean variables, that is pseudo-Boolean constraints. Several SAT encodings of PB constraints have been defined throughout the years. These include the polynomial watchdog encodings [BBR09].

Example 4.13 *In order to impose the at-most-k restriction using the* commander *encoding [FG10], Boolean variables in the scope of the constraint are first arranged into groups of size $g > k$. Next, k auxiliary variables c_{i1} to c_{ik} are introduced for each such group G_i. Subsequently the following three steps are executed:*

- *For each set $S = G_i \cup \{\neg c_{ij} \mid 1 \leq j \leq k\}$ add clauses :*

  - $\bigwedge_{S' \subseteq \{1, \cdots, |S|\}} \bigvee_{m \in S'} \neg x_m$, *where $\sum S' = k + 1$ and $x_m \in S$ for all m;*
  - $\bigwedge_{S' \subseteq \{1, \cdots, |S|\}} \bigvee_{m \in S'} x_m$, *where $\sum S' = |S| - k + 1$ and $x_m \in S$ for all m.*

- *Add clauses $\bigwedge_{j=1}^{k-1} c_{ij} \to c_{i(j+1)}$ to remove symmetrical solutions.*
- *Encode the at-most-k constraint recursively on the commander variables.*

The SAT encoding presented by Bacchus in [Bac07] is a generalisation of the support encoding to non-binary constraints. The interesting thing about this encoding is that running unit propagation on it enforces *generalised-arc-consistency* on the original CSP instance (see Definition 2.15).

Example 4.14 *Bacchus's encoding contains the usual domain clauses, i.e. the at-least-one and at-most-one clauses for each CSP variable v.*

Additionally, for each constraint c new Boolean variables x_{ct} are introduced representing a satisfying tuple t. The constraint clauses are as follows:

-

$$\neg x_{vi} \vee \bigvee_t x_{ct}$$

where each t satisfies $c \in C$ and $(v = i) \in t$
- $x_{vi} \vee \neg x_{ct}$ *for each t satisfying $c \in C$ such that $(v = i) \in t$*

Let $T_c = \{t_1, \cdots, t_l\}$ be a set of satisfying tuples for a constraint c. Note that c is satisfied if and only if one of the t_is is true. Each t_i represents a set of assignments for a fixed set of variables that are constrained by c. Hence, only one of the t_is can be true. Therefore, w.l.o.g., we can add the following set of clauses to Bacchus's encoding for each constraint c:

- at-least-one clause:

$$\bigvee_{t_i \in T_c} x_{ct_i}$$

- at-most-one clauses:

$$\bigwedge_{t_i, t_j \in T_c \,\&\, i \neq j} \neg x_{ct_i} \vee \neg x_{ct_j}$$

We call Bacchus's encoding with additional clauses described above *the extended Bacchus's encoding*.

It turns out that there exists a connection between Bacchus's encoding and a particular graph representation of a CSP instance, namely its hidden variable representation (see Definition 2.7).

Theorem 4.15 *The extended Bacchus's encoding of a CSP instance P is equivalent to the support encoding of the hidden variable representation of P.*

Proof Let $P = (V, D, C)$ be a CSP instance. Let Φ be the extended Bacchus's encoding of P. Let $\Gamma \subset \Phi$ be the largest disjoint set of purely positive clauses. Then Γ contains the following clauses:

- for each variable $v \in V$:

$$\bigvee_{i \in D_v} x_{vi} \,;$$

- for each constraint $c \in C$:

$$\bigvee_{t \text{ satisfies } c} x_{ct} \,.$$

Moreover, by definition, Φ contains the appropriate at-most-one clauses for each $v \in V$ and $c \in C$. All Boolean variables in Φ occur in Γ. Hence, by Lemma 4.6, Φ is a sparse encoding of some CSP $P' = (V', D', C')$. Let γ_c be a CSP variable representing some constraint $c \in C$ and T_c be the set of satisfying tuples for c. Then:

-

$$V' = V \cup \bigcup_{c \in C} \gamma_c \,;$$

-

$$D' = D \cup \bigcup_{c \in C} (D_c = T_c) \,;$$

-

$$C' = \{(v = i \vee \gamma_c \neq t) \mid x_{vi} \vee \neg x_{ct} \in \Phi \} \cup$$

$$\{(v \neq i \vee \bigvee_{t \in T_c} \gamma_c = t) \mid \neg x_{vi} \vee \bigvee_{t \in T_c} x_{ct} \in \Phi \} \,.$$

Note that the primal graph of P' (see Definition 2.3) is a bipartite graph, where there is an edge between two variables if and only if one of them represents a constraint, say c, and the other represents a variable that is in the scope of c. Hence, this graph is the incidence graph of P (see Definition 2.6). Therefore, P' is the hidden variable representation of P. Moreover, as all the constraint clauses of Φ encode binary supports, Φ is the support encoding of P'. $\qquad\square$

Since it is known that establishing arc-consistency on the hidden variable representation of P enforces generalised-arc-consistency on the original problem [SW99], the above theorem also proves that running unit propagation on Bacchus's encoding enforces *generalised-arc-consistency* on the original CSP instance.

4.5 What is a *good* SAT encoding?

Given the large choice of SAT encodings in the literature, it would be useful to clarify which encodings are actually the *good* ones. Identifying those can be quite tricky though.

One desirable feature is that the encoding should be as *compact* as possible. Two common measures for the size of a formula in CNF are: the total number of literals and the number of clauses. However, the most compact encodings can sometimes distort some feature of the given instance that could have been crucial to solving that instance. An example is given in Chapter 7. Therefore, compact encodings do not guarantee better performance.

Another desirable property of a SAT encoding is *high solution density*. It is calculated as the number of solutions divided by 2^n, where n is the number of variables in the encoding. Some evidence was provided in [CFG$^+$96] that if a satisfiable problem has high solution density then a search algorithm might find a solution to such a problem more easily. The log encoding can serve here as a counter-example. It has a logarithmic number of variables in the CSP domain sizes, hence higher SAT solution density than the direct encoding. However, in general the latter was found to help SAT-solvers achieve better performance.

From the point of view of the practitioner a good encoding would allow a SAT-solver to make as many deductions as possible. Since unit propagation underlies any SAT-solver and enforcing local consistency is the key technique in CSP solving, those encodings are good under which unit propagation does as much pruning as possible. In particular, a SAT encoding is regarded as a *good* one if unit propagation achieves generalised-arc-consistency (GAC) (see Definition 2.15) on the original CSP instance.

It is known that unit propagation, for instance, enforces arc-consistency on the *support encoding* of a (binary) CSP instance [Gen02].

Example 4.16 *Let P be a CSP instance defined on two variables v and w, each with domain $\{0, 1, 2\}$. Let P impose just one constraint $v < w$. The support encoding of P is as follows:*

$$x_{v0} \vee x_{v1} \vee x_{v2}, \; x_{w0} \vee x_{w1} \vee x_{w2}$$
$$\neg x_{v0} \vee \neg x_{v1}, \; \neg x_{v0} \vee \neg x_{v2}, \; \neg x_{v1} \vee \neg x_{v2}$$
$$\neg x_{w0} \vee \neg x_{w1}, \; \neg x_{w0} \vee \neg x_{w2}, \; \neg x_{w1} \vee \neg x_{w2}$$

$$\neg x_{v0} \vee x_{w1} \vee x_{w2}$$
$$\neg x_{v1} \vee x_{w2}, \; \neg x_{v2}$$
$$\neg x_{w0}, \; \neg x_{w1} \vee x_{v0}$$
$$\neg x_{w2} \vee x_{v0} \vee x_{v1}$$

where each x_{vi} represents the assignment $v = i$. Unit propagation reduces this set of clauses to:

$$x_{v0} \vee x_{v1}, \; x_{w1} \vee x_{w2}$$
$$\neg x_{v0} \vee \neg x_{v1}, \; \neg x_{w1} \vee \neg x_{w2}$$

$$\neg x_{v0} \vee x_{w1} \vee x_{w2}$$
$$\neg x_{v1} \vee x_{w2}, \; \neg x_{w1} \vee x_{v0}$$
$$\neg x_{w2} \vee x_{v0} \vee x_{v1}$$

Hence, the domain of v is reduced to $\{0, 1\}$ *and the domain of w is reduced to* $\{1, 2\}$. *These are now arc-consistent, since for each possible assignment to v there exists an assignment to w that satisfies the constraint* $v < w$ *(and vice versa)*.

Another example of an encoding on which unit propagation enforces a certain level of consistency is Bacchus's encoding (see Example 4.14). However, this encoding as well as the support encoding are unfortunately often inefficient in practice, since they can produce SAT instances of exponential size.

Since one desirable feature of a SAT encoding is to allow unit propagation to make as many deductions as possible, one might say that an encoding is desirable for which only a few deductions are needed to define the satisfiability of the formula. As SAT-solvers p-simulate (polynomially simulate) general resolution [PD09], this implies that those encodings are desirable that translate a CSP instance into a SAT formula that has a short resolution proof (see Definition 2.20). However, such encodings are not always the best choice in practice, since it might take a lot of time for the solver to find such a proof. A concrete example is given in Chapter 7.

We conclude that there does not seem to be a simple criterion for what makes a good encoding in general. However, we will see in later chapters that in some cases we can identify which encodings are better than others.

4.6 Summary

The remarkable efficiency of SAT-solvers in the last decade has lead to the development of various SAT encodings of CSP instances. Even though such encodings often distort the original structure of the CSP instance, SAT-based constraint solvers frequently outperform conventional CSP-solvers in practice.

The simplest way to encode CSP domains into SAT is to introduce a Boolean variable for each variable-value pair. Examples of such encodings are the direct and the support encoding. The log encoding, on the other hand, introduces a Boolean variable for each bit of the domain of a CSP variable. Another possible way is to encode the domain bounds by introducing variables representing comparisons or intervals. We call such encodings regular and interval-based ones.

The constraints of CSP instances are usually encoded using either the disallowed or allowed variable assignments. Using regular and interval-based encodings one can encode the disallowed (or allowed) regions. Thus the nogoods can be sometimes represented more compactly using such encodings in comparison with the sparse ones.

There exists also a wide range of encodings for specific constraints, like the global cardinality constraint or Pseudo-Boolean constraints. These often introduce some auxiliary variables.

Even though many SAT encodings have been introduced over the years, it is still hard to tell which encodings are actually "good". A few desirable features have been identified, but for each of them counter-examples can be found. It has been proposed, for instance, that a SAT encoding should be: compact, of high solution density, GAC-preserving or have a short resolution proof. Although no one criterion can be identified that would differentiate between a "bad" and "good" encoding for all CSP instances, in the next few chapters we will show that for certain classes of CSP instances it is indeed possible to identify which SAT encoding is actually "good" for *all* instances in a CSP class.

Chapter 5
From CSP to SAT: width restrictions

> *Everything must be taken into account. If the fact will not fit the theory—let the theory go.*
>
> Agatha Christie

In this chapter we draw on a number of recent analytical approaches to try to account for the good performance of general SAT-solvers on many forms of constraint problems. Building on the results of [ABD07, AD08], and [HM05], we show that the power of using k-consistency techniques in a constraint problem is precisely captured by using a single inference rule in a standard Boolean encoding of that problem. We refer to this inference rule as *negative-hyper-resolution*, and show that any conclusions deduced by enforcing k-consistency can be deduced by a sequence of negative-hyper-resolution inferences involving Boolean clauses from the original encoding and negative-hyper-resolvents with at most k literals. Furthermore, by using the approach of [AFT11], and [PD09], we show that current clause-learning SAT-solvers will mimic the effect of such deductions in polynomial expected time, even with a random branching strategy. Hence we show that, although they are not explicitly designed to do so, running a clause-learning SAT-solver on the direct encoding of a constraint problem efficiently simulates the effects of enforcing k-consistency for *all* values of k.

5.1 Preliminaries

In this section we give some background and definitions that will be used throughout the rest of the chapter.

5.1.1 Constraint satisfaction problems and k-consistency

Given any CSP instance (V, D, C), a *partial assignment* is a mapping f from some subset W of V to $\bigcup D_v$ such that $f(v) \in D_v$ for all $v \in W$. A partial assignment

© Springer International Publishing Switzerland 2015

J. Petke, *Bridging Constraint Satisfaction and Boolean Satisfiability*,
Artificial Intelligence: Foundations, Theory, and Algorithms,
DOI 10.1007/978-3-319-21810-6_5

satisfies the constraints of the instance if, for all $(R, (v_1, v_2, \ldots, v_m)) \in C$ such that $v_j \in W$ for $j = 1, 2, \ldots, m$, we have $(f(v_1), f(v_2) \ldots, f(v_m)) \in R$. A partial assignment that satisfies the constraints of an instance is called a *partial solution*[1] to that instance. The set of variables on which a partial assignment f is defined is called the domain of f, and denoted $Dom(f)$. A partial solution g *extends* a partial solution f if $Dom(f) \subseteq Dom(g)$ and $g(v) = f(v)$ for all $v \in Dom(f)$. A partial solution with domain V is called a *solution*.

As mentioned in Section 2.2.2, one way to derive new information about a CSP instance, which may help to determine whether or not it has a solution, is to use some form of constraint propagation to enforce some level of *local consistency* [Bes06]. For example, it is possible to use the notion of *k-consistency* (see Definition 2.13). We note that there are several different but equivalent ways to define and enforce k-consistency described in the literature [Bes06, Coo89, Fre78]. Our presentation follows that of [ABD07], which is inspired by the notion of existential k-pebble games introduced in [KV00b].

Definition 5.1 *[ABD07] For any CSP instance P, the k-consistency closure of P is the set H of partial assignments which is obtained by the following algorithm:*

1. *let H be the collection of all partial solutions f of P with $|Dom(f)| \leq k + 1$;*
2. *for every $f \in H$ with $|Dom(f)| \leq k$ and every variable v of P, if there is no $g \in H$ such that g extends f and $v \in Dom(g)$, then remove f and all its extensions from H;*
3. *repeat step 2 until H is unchanged.*

Note that computing the k-consistency closure according to this definition corresponds precisely to enforcing *strong $(k + 1)$-consistency* according to Definition 2.13.

Throughout this book, we assume that the domain of possible values for each variable in a CSP instance is finite. It is straightforward to show that for any fixed k, and any fixed maximum domain size, the k-consistency closure of an instance P can be computed in polynomial-time [ABD07, Coo89].

Note that any solution to P must extend some element of the k-consistency closure of P. Hence, if the k-consistency closure of P is empty, for some k, then P has no solutions. The converse is not true in general, but it holds for certain special cases, such as the class of instances whose structure has tree-width bounded by k [ABD07], or the class of instances whose constraint relations are *0/1/all* relations (see Section 3.4) , or *connected-row-convex* relations (see Section 3.5). For these special kinds of instances it is possible to determine in polynomial-time whether or not a solution exists simply by computing the k-consistency closure, for an appropriate choice of k. Moreover, if a solution exists, then it can be constructed in polynomial-time by selecting each variable in turn, assigning each possible value,

---

[1]Note that not all partial solutions extend to solutions.

re-computing the k-consistency closure, and retaining an assignment that gives a non-empty result.

The following result gives a useful condition for determining whether the k-consistency closure of a CSP instance is empty.

Lemma 5.2 *[KV00b] The k-consistency closure of a CSP instance P is non-empty if and only if there exists a non-empty family H of partial solutions to P such that:*

1. *if $f \in H$, then $|Dom(f)| \leq k + 1$;*
2. *if $f \in H$ and f extends g, then $g \in H$;*
3. *if $f \in H$, $|Dom(f)| \leq k$, and $v \notin Dom(f)$ is a variable of P, then there is some $g \in H$ such that g extends f and $v \in Dom(g)$.*

A set of partial solutions H satisfying the conditions described in Lemma 5.2 is sometimes called a *strategy* for the instance P [BK09, KV00b].

5.1.2 Inference rules

In the next section, we shall establish a close connection between the k-consistency algorithm and a form of inference called negative-hyper-resolution [BL99], which we define as follows:

Definition 5.3 *If we have a collection of clauses of the form $C_i \vee \neg x_i$, for $i = 1, 2, \ldots, r$, and a clause $C_0 \vee x_1 \vee x_2 \vee \cdots \vee x_r$, where each x_i is a Boolean variable, and C_0 and each C_i is a (possibly empty) disjunction of* negative *literals, then we can deduce the clause $C_0 \vee C_1 \vee \cdots \vee C_r$.*

We call this form of inference negative-hyper-resolution *and the resultant clause $C_0 \vee C_1 \vee \cdots \vee C_r$ the* negative-hyper-resolvent.

In the case where C_0 is empty, the negative-hyper-resolution rule is equivalent to the nogood resolution rule described in [HM05] as well as the H5-k rule introduced in [dK89] and the nogood recording scheme described in [SV93].

Note that the inference obtained by negative-hyper-resolution can also be obtained by a sequence of standard resolution steps. However, the reason for introducing negative-hyper-resolution is that it allows us to deduce the clauses we need in a single step without needing to introduce intermediate clauses (which may contain up to $r - 1$ more literals than the negative-hyper-resolvent). By restricting the size of the clauses we use in this way we are able to obtain better performance bounds for SAT-solvers in the results below.

Example 5.4 *Assume we have a collection of clauses of the form $C_i \vee \neg x_i$, for $i = 1, 2, \ldots, r$, and a clause $C_0 \vee x_1 \vee x_2 \vee \cdots \vee x_r$, as specified in Definition 5.3, where each $C_i = C_0$. The negative-hyper-resolvent of this set of clauses is C_0.*

The clause C_0 can also be obtained by a sequence of standard resolution steps, as follows. First resolve $C_0 \vee x_1 \vee x_2 \vee \cdots \vee x_r$ with $C_0 \vee \neg x_r$ to obtain $C_0 \vee x_1 \vee x_2 \vee \cdots \vee x_{r-1}$. Then resolve this with the next clause, $C_0 \vee \neg x_{r-1}$, and so on for *the other clauses, until finally we obtain C_0. However, in this case the intermediate clause $C_0 \vee x_1 \vee x_2 \vee \cdots \vee x_{r-1}$ contains $r - 1$ more literals than the negative-hyper-resolvent.*

Example 5.5 *Note that the nogood clauses in the direct encoding of a binary CSP instance can each be obtained by a single negative-hyper-resolution step from an appropriate support clause in the support encoding together with an appropriate collection of at-most-one clauses. Let $A \subseteq D_w$ be the set of values for the variable w which are compatible with the assignment $v = i$, then the support encoding will contain the clause $C = \neg x_{vi} \vee \bigvee_{j \in A} x_{wj}$. If there are any values $k \in D_w$ which are incompatible with the assignment $v = i$, then we can form the negative-hyper-resolvent of C with the at-most-one clauses $\neg x_{wk} \vee \neg x_{wj}$ for each $j \in A$, to obtain the corresponding nogood clause, $\neg x_{vi} \vee \neg x_{wk}$.*

A negative-hyper-resolution *derivation* of a clause C from a set of initial clauses Φ is a sequence of clauses $C_1, C_2, \ldots, C_m$, where $C_m = C$ and each C_i follows by the negative-hyper-resolution rule from some collection of clauses, each of which is either contained in Φ or else occurs earlier in the sequence. The *width* of this derivation is defined to be the maximum size of any of the clauses C_i. If C_m is the empty clause, then we say that the derivation is a *negative-hyper-resolution refutation* of Φ.

5.2 *k*-consistency and negative-hyper-resolution

It has been pointed out by many authors that enforcing local consistency is a form of inference on relations analogous to the use of the resolution rule on clauses [Bac07, Bes06, HM05, RD00]. The precise strength of the standard resolution inference rule on the direct encoding of a CSP instance was considered in [Wal00], where it was shown that *unit* resolution (where one of the clauses being resolved consists of a single literal), corresponds to enforcing a weak form of local consistency known as *forward checking*. In [HM05] it was pointed out that the standard resolution rule with no restriction on clause length is able to simulate all the inferences made by a k-consistency algorithm. In [AD08] it was shown that the standard resolution rule restricted to clauses with at most k literals, known as the k resolution rule, can be characterised in terms of the Boolean existential $(k + 1)$-pebble game. It follows that on CSP instances with Boolean domains this form of inference corresponds to enforcing k-consistency. An alternative proof that k-resolution achieves k-consistency for instances with Boolean domains is given in [Hoo07, Thm. 3.22].

Here we extend these results a little, to show that for CSP instances with arbitrary finite domains, applying the negative-hyper-resolution rule on the direct encoding to obtain clauses with at most k literals corresponds precisely to enforcing k-consistency. A similar relationship was stated in [dK89], but a complete proof was not given.

Note that the bound, k, that we impose on the size of the negative-hyper-resolvents, is independent of the domain size. In other words, using this inference rule we only need to consider inferred clauses of size at most k, even though we make use of clauses in the encoding whose size is equal to the domain size, which may be arbitrarily large.

Theorem 5.6 *The k-consistency closure of a CSP instance P is empty if and only if its direct encoding as a set of clauses has a negative-hyper-resolution refutation of width at most k.*

The proof is broken down into two lemmas inspired by Lemmas 2 and 3 in [AD08].

Lemma 5.7 *Let P be a CSP instance, and let Φ be its direct encoding as a set of clauses. If Φ has no negative-hyper-resolution refutation of width k or less, then the k-consistency closure of P is non-empty.*

Proof Let V be the set of variables of P, where each $v \in V$ has domain D_v, and let $X = \{x_{vi} \mid v \in V, i \in D_v\}$ be the corresponding set of Boolean variables in Φ. Let Γ be the set of all clauses having a negative-hyper-resolution derivation from Φ of width at most k. By the definition of negative-hyper-resolution, every non-empty clause in Γ consists entirely of negative literals.

Now let H be the set of all partial assignments for P with domain size at most $k + 1$ that do not falsify any clause in $\Phi \cup \Gamma$ under the direct encoding.

Consider any element $f \in H$. By the definition of H, f does not falsify any clause of Φ, so by the definition of the direct encoding, every element of H is a partial solution to P. Furthermore, if f extends g, then g is also an element of H, because g makes fewer assignments than f and hence cannot falsify any additional clauses to f.

If Φ has no negative-hyper-resolution refutation of width at most k, then Γ does not contain the empty clause, so H contains (at least) the partial solution with empty domain, and hence H is not empty.

Now let f be any element of H with $|Dom(f)| \leq k$ and let v be any variable of P that is not in $Dom(f)$. For any partial assignment g that extends f and has $Dom(g) = Dom(f) \cup \{v\}$ we have that either $g \in H$ or else there exists a clause in $\Phi \cup \Gamma$ that is falsified by g. Since g is a partial assignment, any clause C in $\Phi \cup \Gamma$ that is falsified by g, must consist entirely of negative literals. Hence the literals of C must either be of the form $\neg x_{wf(w)}$ for some $w \in Dom(f)$, or else $\neg x_{vg(v)}$. Moreover, any such clause must contain the literal $\neg x_{vg(v)}$, or else it would already be falsified by f.

Assume, for contradiction, that H does not contain any assignment g that extends f and has $Dom(g) = Dom(f) \cup \{v\}$. In that case, we have that, for each $i \in D_v$, $\Phi \cup \Gamma$ contains a clause C_i consisting of negative literals of the form $\neg x_{wf(w)}$ for some $w \in Dom(f)$, together with the literal $\neg x_{vi}$. Now consider the clause, C, which is the negative-hyper-resolvent of these clauses C_i and the at-least-one clause $\bigvee_{i \in D_v} x_{vi}$. The clause C consists entirely of negative literals of the form $\neg x_{wf(w)}$ for some $w \in Dom(f)$, so it has width at most $|Dom(f)| \leq k$, and hence is an element of Γ.

However C is falsified by f, which contradicts the choice of f. Hence we have shown that for all $f \in H$ with $|Dom(f)| \leq k$, and for all variables v such that $v \notin Dom(f)$, there is some $g \in H$ such that g extends f and $v \in Dom(g)$.

We have shown that H satisfies all the conditions required by Lemma 5.2, so we conclude that the k-consistency closure of P is non-empty. $\square$

Lemma 5.8 *Let P be a CSP instance, and let Φ be its direct encoding as a set of clauses. If the k-consistency closure of P is non-empty, then Φ has no negative-hyper-resolution refutation of width k or less.*

Proof Let V be the set of variables of P, where each $v \in V$ has domain D_v, and let $X = \{x_{vi} \mid v \in V, i \in D_v\}$ be the corresponding set of Boolean variables in Φ.

By Lemma 5.2, if the k-consistency closure of P is non-empty, then there exists a non-empty set H of partial solutions to P which satisfies the three properties described in Lemma 5.2.

Now consider any negative-hyper-resolution derivation Γ from Φ of width at most k. We show by induction on the length of this derivation that the elements of H do not falsify any clause in the derivation. First we note that the elements of H are partial solutions, so they satisfy all the constraints of P, and hence do not falsify any clause of Φ. This establishes the base case. Assume, for induction, that all clauses in the derivation earlier than some clause C are not falsified by any element of H.

Note that, apart from the at-least-one clauses, all clauses in Φ and Γ consist entirely of negative literals. Hence we may assume, without loss of generality, that C is the negative-hyper-resolvent of a set of clauses $\Delta = \{C_i \vee \neg x_{vi} \mid i \in D_v\}$ and the at-least-one clause $\bigvee_{i \in D_v} x_{vi}$, for some fixed variable v.

If $f \in H$ falsifies C, then the literals of C must all be of the form $\neg x_{wf(w)}$, for some $w \in Dom(f)$. Since the width of the derivation is at most k, C contains at most k literals, and hence we may assume that $|Dom(f)| \leq k$. But then, by the choice of H, there must exist some extension g of f in H such that $v \in Dom(g)$. Any such g will falsify some clause in Δ, which contradicts our inductive hypothesis. Hence no $f \in H$ falsifies C, and, in particular, C cannot be empty.

It follows that no negative-hyper-resolution derivation of width at most k can contain the empty clause. $\square$

Note that the proof of Theorem 5.6 applies to any sparse encoding that contains the at-least-one clauses for each variable, and where all other clauses are purely negative. We will call such an encoding a *negative sparse encoding*. As well as the direct encoding, other negative sparse encodings exist. For example, we may use negative clauses that involve only a subset of the variables in the scope of some constraints (to forbid tuples where all possible extensions to the complete scope are disallowed by the constraint). Another example of a negative sparse encoding is the multivalued direct encoding (see Section 4.1).

Corollary 5.9 *The k-consistency closure of a CSP instance P is empty if and only if any negative sparse encoding of P has a negative-hyper-resolution refutation of width at most k.*

5.3   Negative-hyper-resolution and SAT-solvers

In this section we adapt the machinery from [AFT11], and [PD09] to show that for any fixed k, the existence of a negative-hyper-resolution refutation of width k is likely to be discovered by a SAT-solver in polynomial-time using standard clause learning and restart techniques, even with a totally random branching strategy.

Note that previous results about the power of clause-learning SAT-solvers have generally assumed an optimal branching strategy [BKS04, PD09] — they have shown what solvers are potentially capable of doing, rather than what they are likely to achieve in practice. An important exception is [AFT11], which gives an analysis of likely behaviour, but relies on the existence of a standard resolution proof of bounded-width. Here we show that the results of [AFT11] can be extended to hyper-resolution proofs, which can be shorter and narrower than their associated standard resolution proofs.

We will make use of the following terminology from [AFT11]. For a clause C, a Boolean variable x, and a truth value $a \in \{0, 1\}$, the restriction of C by the assignment $x = a$, denoted $C|_{x=a}$, is defined to be the constant $\mathbf{1}$, if the assignment satisfies the clause, or else the clause obtained by deleting from C any literals involving the variable x. For any sequence of assignments S of the form $(x_1 = a_1, x_2 = a_2, \ldots, x_r = a_r)$ we write $C|_S$ to denote the result of computing the restriction of C by each assignment in turn. If $C|_S$ is empty, then we say that the assignments in S *falsify* the clause C. For a set of clauses Δ, we write $\Delta|_S$ to denote the set $\{C|_S \mid C \in \Delta\} \setminus \{\mathbf{1}\}$.

Most current SAT-solvers operate in the following way [AFT11, PD09]. They maintain a database of clauses Δ and a current state S, which is a partial assignment of truth values to the Boolean variables in the clauses of Δ. A high-level description of the algorithms used to update the clause database and the state, derived from the description given in [AFT11], is shown in Algorithm 5.1[2] (a similar framework, using slightly different terminology, is given in [PD09]).

Now consider a run of the algorithm shown in Algorithm 5.1, started with the initial database Δ, and the empty state S_0, until it either halts or discovers a *conflict* (i.e., $\emptyset \in \Delta|_S$). Such a run is called a *complete round started with* Δ, and we represent it by the sequence of states $S_0, \ldots, S_m$, that the algorithm maintains. Note that each state S_i extends the state S_{i-1} by a single assignment to a Boolean variable, which may be either a *decision assignment* or an *implied assignment*.

More generally, a *round* is an initial segment $S_0, S_1, \ldots, S_r$ of a complete round started with Δ, up to a state S_r such that either $\Delta|_{S_r}$ contains the empty clause, or $\Delta|_{S_r}$ does not contain any unit clause. For any clause C, we say that a round $S_0, S_1, \ldots, S_r$ satisfies C if $C|_{S_r} = \mathbf{1}$, and we say that the round falsifies C if $C|_{S_r}$ is empty.

---

[2]Note that this conflict-driven clause learning (CDCL) algorithm is still based on the core DPLL algorithm (see Algorithm 2.2 for comparison).

Algorithm 5.1 Framework for a typical clause-learning SAT-solver

---

Input: Δ : set of clauses;
       S : partial assignment of truth values to variables.

1. **while** $\Delta|_S \neq \emptyset$ **do**
2.   **if** $\emptyset \in \Delta|_S$ **then**   Conflict
3.   **if** S contains no decision assignments **then**
4.   **print** "UNSATISFIABLE" and halt
5.   **else**
6.   apply the *learning scheme* to add a new clause to Δ
7.   **if** *restart policy* says restart **then**
8.   set $S = \emptyset$
9.   **else**
10.   select most recent conflict-causing unreversed decision assignment in S
11.   reverse this decision, and remove all later assignments from S
12.   **end if**
13.   **end if**
14.   **else if** $\{l\} \in \Delta|_S$ for some literal l **then**   Unit Propagation
15.   add to S the *implied assignment* $x = a$ which satisfies l
16.   **else**   Decision
17.   apply the *branching strategy* to choose a *decision assignment* $x = a$
18.   add this decision assignment to S
19.   **end if**
20. **end while**
21. **print** "SATISFIABLE" and output S

If $S_0, S_1, \ldots, S_r$ is a round started with Δ, and $\Delta|_{S_r}$ contains the empty clause, then the algorithm either reports unsatisfiability or learns a new clause: such a round is called *conclusive*. If a round is not conclusive we call it *inconclusive*[3]. Note that if $S_0, S_1, \ldots, S_r$ is an inconclusive round started with Δ, then $\Delta|_{S_r}$ does not contain the empty clause, and does not contain any unit clauses. Hence, for any clause $C \in \Delta$, if S_r falsifies all the literals of C except one, then it must satisfy the remaining literal, and hence satisfy C. This property of clauses is captured by the following definition.

Definition 5.10 *[AFT11] Let Δ be a set of clauses, C a non-empty clause, and l a literal of C. We say that Δ absorbs C at l if every inconclusive round started with Δ that falsifies $C \setminus \{l\}$ satisfies C.*

If Δ absorbs C at each literal l in C, then we simply say that Δ absorbs C.

If C is in the set Δ then it is always absorbed (see Lemma 5.14), but clauses that are not in Δ may also be absorbed in some cases. We will see an example of this situation in Example 5.11.

Note that a closely related notion is introduced in [PD09] for clauses that are *not* absorbed by a set of clauses Δ; they are referred to as *1-empowering* with respect

---

[3]Note that a complete round that assigns all variables and reports satisfiability is called inconclusive.

to Δ. (The exact relationship between 1-empowering and absorption is discussed in [AFT11].)

We will now explore the relationship between absorption and negative-hyper-resolution.

Example 5.11 *Let Δ be the direct encoding of a CSP instance $P = (V, D, C)$, where $V = \{u, v, w\}$, $D_u = D_v = D_w = \{1, 2\}$ and C contains two binary constraints: one forbids the assignment of the value 1 to u and v simultaneously, and the other forbids the simultaneous assignment of the value 2 to u and 1 to w. Let C also contain a ternary constraint that forbids the assignment of the value 2 to all three variables simultaneously.*

$$\Delta = \{\, x_{u1} \vee x_{u2},\ x_{v1} \vee x_{v2},\ x_{w1} \vee x_{w2},$$

$$\neg x_{u1} \vee \neg x_{u2},\ \neg x_{v1} \vee \neg x_{v2},\ \neg x_{w1} \vee \neg x_{w2},$$

$$\neg x_{u1} \vee \neg x_{v1},\ \neg x_{u2} \vee \neg x_{w1},\ \neg x_{u2} \vee \neg x_{v2} \vee \neg x_{w2} \,\}.$$

The clause $\neg x_{v1} \vee \neg x_{w1}$ is not contained in Δ, but can be obtained by negative-hyper-resolution from the clauses $x_{u1} \vee x_{u2}, \neg x_{u1} \vee \neg x_{v1}, \neg x_{u2} \vee \neg x_{w1}$.

This clause is absorbed by Δ, since every inconclusive round that sets $x_{v1} = True$ must set $x_{w1} = False$ by unit propagation, and every inconclusive round that sets $x_{w1} = True$ must set $x_{v1} = False$ also by unit propagation.

Example 5.11 indicates that clauses that can be obtained by negative hyper-resolution from a set of clauses Δ are sometimes absorbed by Δ. The next result clarifies when this situation holds.

Lemma 5.12 *Any negative-hyper-resolvent of a set of disjoint clauses is absorbed by that set of clauses.*

Proof Let C be the negative-hyper-resolvent of a set of clauses $\Delta = \{C_i \vee \neg x_i \mid i = 1, 2, \ldots, r\}$ and a clause $C' = C_0 \vee x_1 \vee x_2 \vee \cdots \vee x_r$, where each C_i is a (possibly empty) disjunction of negative literals, for $0 \le i \le r$. Then $C = C_0 \vee C_1 \vee \cdots \vee C_r$ by Definition 5.3. By Definition 5.10, we must show that $\Delta \cup C'$ absorbs C at each of its literals. Assume all but one of the literals of C are falsified. Since the set of clauses $\Delta \cup C'$ are assumed to be disjoint, the remaining literal l must belong to exactly one of the clauses in this set. There are two cases to consider.

1. If l belongs to the clause C', then all clauses in Δ have all but one literals falsified, so the remaining literal $\neg x_i$ in each of these clauses is set to *True*, by unit propagation. Hence all literals in C' are falsified, except for l, so l is set to *True*, by unit propagation.
2. If l belongs to one of the clauses $C_i \vee \neg x_i$, then all of the remaining clauses in Δ have all but one literals falsified, so the corresponding literals $\neg x_j$ are set to *True*, by unit propagation. Hence all literals in C' are falsified, except for x_i, so x_i is set to *True*, by unit propagation. But now all literals in $C_i \vee \neg x_i$ are falsified, except for l, so l is set to *True* by unit propagation. □

We note here that if Δ absorbs a non-empty clause C, then every satisfying assignment of Δ satisfies C, that is, C is implied by Δ (see Lemma 4 in [AFT11]). The converse is not true. The next example shows that the negative-hyper-resolvent of a set of clauses that is *not* disjoint will *not* necessarily be absorbed by those clauses.

Example 5.13 *Recall the set of clauses Δ given in Example 5.11, which is the direct encoding of a CSP instance with three variables $\{u, v, w\}$, each with domain $\{1, 2\}$.*

The clause $\neg x_{u2} \vee \neg x_{v2}$ is not contained in Δ, but can be obtained by negative-hyper-resolution from the clauses $x_{w1} \vee x_{w2}, \neg x_{u2} \vee \neg x_{v2} \vee \neg x_{w2}, \neg x_{u2} \vee \neg x_{w1}$.

This clause is not *absorbed by Δ, since an inconclusive round that sets $x_{v2} = $ True will not necessarily ensure that $x_{u2} = $ False by unit propagation.*

The basic approach we shall use to establish our main results below is to show that any clauses that can be obtained by bounded-width negative-hyper-resolution from a given set of clauses, but are not immediately absorbed (such as the one in Example 5.13), are likely to become absorbed quite quickly because of the additional clauses that are added by the process of clause learning. Hence a clause-learning SAT-solver is likely to fairly rapidly absorb all of the clauses that can be derived from its original database of clauses by negative-hyper-resolution. In particular, if the empty clause can be derived by negative-hyper-resolution, then the solver will fairly rapidly absorb some literal and its complement, and hence report unsatisfiability (see the proof of Theorem 5.17 for details).

The following key properties of absorption are established in [AFT11].

Lemma 5.14 *[AFT11] Let Δ and Δ' be sets of clauses, and let C and C' be non-empty clauses.*

1. *If C belongs to Δ, then Δ absorbs C;*
2. *If $C \subseteq C'$ and Δ absorbs C, then Δ absorbs C';*
3. *If $\Delta \subseteq \Delta'$ and Δ absorbs C, then Δ' absorbs C.*

Note that the second property in Lemma 5.14 implies that a SAT-solver can absorb a clause C even if the learning scheme does not directly add it.

To allow further analysis, we need to make some assumptions about the *learning scheme*, the *restart policy* and the *branching strategy* used by our SAT-solver (for more details on the core algorithm of modern SAT-solvers see Section 2.3).

Assumption 5.15 *The learning scheme chooses an* asserting clause *(see Definition 2.24).*

Most learning schemes in current use satisfy this assumption [PD09, ZMMM01], including the learning schemes called 1UIP (or FirstUIP, see Section 2.4.3) and Decision [ZMMM01].

We make no particular assumption about the restart policy. However, our main result is phrased in terms of a bound on the expected number of restarts. If the algorithm restarts after r conflicts, our bound on the expected number of restarts can simply be multiplied by r to get a bound on the expected number of conflicts. This means that the results will be strongest if the algorithm restarts *immediately after each conflict*. In that case, $r = 1$ and our bound will also bound the expected number of conflicts. Existing SAT-solvers typically do not employ such an aggressive restart policy, but we note the remark in [PD09] that "there has been a clear trend towards more and more frequent restarts for modern SAT solvers".

The branching strategy determines which decision assignment is chosen after an inconclusive round that is not complete. In most current SAT-solvers the strategy is based on some heuristic measure of *variable activity*, which is related to the occurrence of a variable in conflict clauses [MMZ⁺01]. However, to simplify the probabilistic analysis, we will make the following assumption.

Assumption 5.16 *The branching strategy chooses a variable uniformly at random amongst the unassigned variables, and assigns it the value True.*

As noted in [AFT11], the same analysis we give below can also be applied to any other branching strategy that randomly chooses between making a heuristic-based decision or a randomly based decision. More precisely, if we allow, say, $c > 1$ rounds of non-random decisions between random ones, then the number of required restarts and conflicts would appear multiplied by a factor of c.

An algorithm that behaves according to the description in Algorithm 5.1, and satisfies the assumptions above, will be called a *standard randomised* SAT-solver.

Theorem 5.17 *If a set of non-empty clauses Δ over n Boolean variables has a negative-hyper-resolution refutation of width k and length m, then the expected number of restarts required by a standard randomised SAT-solver to discover that Δ is unsatisfiable is less than $mnk^2 \binom{n}{k}$.*

Proof Let $C_1, C_2, \ldots, C_m$ be a negative-hyper-resolution refutation of width k from Δ, where C_m is the first occurrence of the empty clause. Since each clause in Δ is non-empty, C_m must be derived by negative-hyper-resolution from some collection of negative literals $\neg x_1, \neg x_2, \ldots \neg x_d$ and a purely positive clause $x_1 \vee x_2 \vee \cdots \vee x_d \in \Delta$.

Now consider a standard randomised SAT-solver started with database Δ. Once all of the unit clauses $\neg x_i$ are absorbed by the current database, then, by Definition 5.10, any further inconclusive round of the algorithm must assign all variables x_i false, and hence falsify the clause $x_1 \vee x_2 \vee \cdots x_d$. Since this happens even when no decision assignments are made, the SAT-solver will report unsatisfiability.

It only remains to bound the expected number of restarts required until each clause C_i is absorbed, for $1 \leq i < m$. Let each C_i be the negative-hyper-resolvent of clauses $C_{i1}, C_{i2}, \ldots, C_{ir}$, each of the form $C'_{ij} \vee \neg x_j$, together with a clause $C_{i0} = C_0 \vee x_1 \vee x_2 \vee \cdots \vee x_r$ from Δ, where C_0 is a (possibly empty) disjunction of negative literals. Assume also that each clause C_{ij} is absorbed by Δ for $j = 0, 1, \ldots, r$.

If Δ absorbs C_i, then no further learning or restarts are needed, so assume now that Δ does not absorb C_i. By Definition 5.10, this means that there exists some literal l and some inconclusive round R started with Δ that falsifies $C_i \setminus \{l\}$ and does not satisfy C_i. Note that R must leave the literal l unassigned, because one assignment would satisfy C_i and the other would falsify C_0 and each C'_{ij}, and hence force all of the literals $\neg x_j$ used in the negative-hyper-resolution step to be satisfied, because each C_{ij} is absorbed by Δ, so C_{i0} would be falsified, contradicting the fact that R is inconclusive.

Hence, if the branching strategy chooses to falsify the literals $C_i \setminus \{l\}$ whenever it has a choice, it will construct an inconclusive round R' where l is unassigned (since all the decision assignments in R' are also assigned the same values in R, any implied assignments in R' must also be assigned the same values[4] in R, but we have shown that R leaves l unassigned). If the branching strategy then chooses to falsify the remaining literal l of C_i, then the algorithm would construct a conclusive round R'' where C_{i0} is falsified, and all decision assignments falsify literals in C_i. Hence, by Assumption 5.15, the algorithm would then learn some asserting clause C' and add it to Δ to obtain a new set Δ'.

Since C' is an asserting clause, it contains exactly one literal, l', that is falsified at the highest level in R''. Hence, any inconclusive round R started with Δ' that falsifies $C_i \setminus \{l\}$ will falsify all but one literal of C', and hence force the remaining literal l' to be satisfied, by unit propagation. If this new implied assignment for l' propagates to force l to be true, then R satisfies C_i, and hence Δ' absorbs C_i at l. If not, then the branching strategy can once again choose to falsify the remaining literal l of C_i, which will cause a new asserting clause to be learned and added to Δ. Since each new asserting clause forces a new literal to be satisfied after falsifying $C_i \setminus \{l\}$ this process can be repeated fewer than n times before it is certain that Δ' absorbs C_i at l.

Now consider any sequence of k random branching choices. If the first $k - 1$ of these each falsify a literal of $C_i \setminus \{l\}$, and the final choice falsifies l, then we have shown that the associated round will reach a conflict, and add an asserting clause to Δ. With a random branching strategy, as described in Assumption 5.16, the probability that this happens is at least the probability that the first $k - 1$ random choices consist of a fixed set of variables (in some order), and the final choice is the variable associated with l. The number of random choices that fall in a fixed set follows the hypergeometric distribution, so the overall probability of this is $\frac{1}{\binom{n}{k-1}} \frac{1}{(n-k+1)} = 1/(k\binom{n}{k})$.

To obtain an upper bound on the expected number of restarts, consider the worst case where we require n asserting clauses to be added to absorb each clause C_i at each of its k literals l. Since we require only an upper bound, we will treat each round as an independent trial with success probability $p = 1/(k\binom{n}{k})$, and consider the worst case where we have to achieve $(m - 1)nk$ successes to ensure that C_i for $1 \le i < m$ is absorbed. In this case the total number of restarts will follow a negative binomial distribution, with expected value $(m - 1)nk/p$. Hence in all cases the expected number of restarts is less than $mnk^2\binom{n}{k}$.   □

---

[4]See Lemma 2 in [AFT11] for a more formal statement and proof of this assertion.

A tighter bound on the number of restarts can be obtained if we focus on the Decision learning scheme [AFT11, ZMMM01], as the next result indicates.

Definition 5.18 *The conflict clause added by the Decision learning scheme contains precisely the decision variables involved in the conflict.*

Theorem 5.19 *If a set of non-empty clauses Δ over n Boolean variables has a negative-hyper-resolution refutation of width k and length m, then the expected number of restarts required by a standard randomised SAT-solver using the Decision learning scheme to discover that Δ is unsatisfiable is less than $m\binom{n}{k}$.*

Proof The proof is similar to the proof of Theorem 5.17, except that the Decision learning scheme has the additional feature that the literals in the chosen conflict clause falsify a subset of the current decision assignments. Hence in the situation we consider, where the decision assignments all falsify literals of some clause C_i, this learning scheme will learn a subset of C_i, and hence immediately absorb C_i, by Lemma 5.14 (1,2). Hence the maximum number of learnt clauses required is reduced from $(m-1)nk$ to $(m-1)$, and the probability is increased from $1/(k\binom{n}{k})$ to $1/\binom{n}{k}$, giving the tighter bound. $\qquad\square$

Note that a similar argument shows that the standard deviation of the number of restarts is less than the standard deviation of a negative binomial distribution with parameters m and $1/\binom{n}{k}$, which is less than $\sqrt{m}\binom{n}{k}$. Hence, by Chebyshev's inequality (one-tailed version), the probability that a standard randomised SAT-solver using the Decision learning scheme will discover that Δ is unsatisfiable after $(m+\sqrt{m})\binom{n}{k}$ restarts is greater than $1/2$.

5.4 *k*-consistency and SAT-solvers

By combining Theorem 5.6 and Theorem 5.19 we obtain the following result linking *k*-consistency and SAT-solvers.

Theorem 5.20 *If the k-consistency closure of a CSP instance P is empty, then the expected number of restarts required by a standard randomised SAT-solver using the Decision learning scheme to discover that the direct encoding of P is unsatisfiable is $O(n^{2k}d^{2k})$, where n is the number of variables in P and d is the maximum domain size.*

Proof The length m of a negative-hyper-resolution refutation of width k is bounded by the number of possible nogoods of length at most k for P, which is $\sum_{i=1}^{k} d^i\binom{n}{i}$. Hence, by Theorem 5.6 and Theorem 5.19 we obtain a bound of $\left(\sum_{i=1}^{k} d^i\binom{n}{i}\right)\binom{nd}{k}$, which is $O(n^{2k}d^{2k})$. $\qquad\square$

Hence a standard randomised SAT-solver with a suitable learning strategy will decide the satisfiability of any CSP instance with tree-width k with $O(n^{2k}d^{2k})$

expected restarts, even when it is set to restart immediately after each conflict. In particular, the satisfiability of any tree-structured binary CSP instance (i.e., with tree-width 1) will be decided by such a solver with at most $O(n^2d^2)$ expected conflicts, which is comparable with the growth rate of an optimal arc-consistency algorithm for binary constraints. Note that this result cannot be obtained directly from [AFT11], because the direct encoding of an instance with tree-width k is a set of clauses whose tree-width may be as high as dk.

Moreover, a standard randomised SAT-solver will decide the satisfiability of any CSP instance, with any structure, within the same polynomial bounds, if the constraint relations satisfy certain algebraic properties that ensure bounded-width [BK09]. Examples of such constraint types include the 0/1/all relations and the connected-row-convex relations, which can both be decided by 2-consistency.

It was shown in [Gen02] that the support encoding of a binary CSP instance can be made arc-consistent (that is, 1-consistent) by applying unit propagation alone. Hence, a standard SAT-solver will mimic the effect of enforcing arc-consistency on such an encoding before making any decisions or restarts. By combining Theorem 5.20 with the observation in Example 5.5 that the direct encoding can be obtained from the support encoding by negative-hyper-resolution, we obtain the following corollary concerning the support encoding for all higher levels of consistency.

Corollary 5.21 *For any $k \geq 2$, if the k-consistency closure of a binary CSP instance P is empty, then the expected number of restarts required by a standard randomised SAT-solver using the Decision learning scheme to discover that the support encoding of P is unsatisfiable is $O(n^{2k}d^{2k})$, where n is the number of variables in P and d is the maximum domain size.*

The CSP literature describes many variations on the notion of consistency. In this chapter we have considered k-consistency only. We note that our results can be generalised to some other types of consistency such as singleton arc-consistency [Bes06]. The extension to singleton arc-consistency follows from the recent discovery that if a family of CSP instances is solvable by enforcing singleton arc-consistency, then the instances have bounded-width [CDG11]. In other words, all such instances can be solved by enforcing k-consistency, for some fixed k. Hence, by Theorem 5.20, their direct encoding will be solved in polynomial expected time by a standard randomised SAT-solver.

5.5   Experimental results

The polynomial upper bounds we obtain in this chapter are not asymptotic, they apply for all values of n, m and k. However, they are very conservative, and are likely to be met very easily in practice.

To investigate how an existing SAT-solver actually performs, we measured the runtime of the MiniSAT solver [ES03], version 2.2.0, on a family of CSP instances that can be decided by a fixed level of consistency. For comparison, we also ran our experiments on two state-of-the-art constraint solvers: we used Minion [GJM06], version 0.12, and the G12 finite domain solver [NSB+07], version 1.4.

To match the simplified assumptions of our analysis more closely, we ran a further set of experiments on a core version of MiniSAT in order to get a solver that uses only unit propagation and conflict-directed learning with restarts. We also modified the solver to follow the random branching strategy described above. Our solver does not delete any learnt clauses and uses an extreme restart policy that makes it restart whenever it encounters a conflict. It uses the same learning scheme as MiniSAT. We refer to this modified solver as simple-MiniSAT.

As the characteristic feature of the instances tested is their relatively low tree-width, we also used the Toulbar2 solver [SBdG+08]. This solver implements the BTD (Backtracking with Tree-Decomposition) technique which has been shown to be efficient in practice, in contrast to earlier methods that had been proposed to attempt to exploit tree-decompositions of the input problem [JT03]. As the problem of finding a tree-decomposition of minimal width (i.e., the tree-width) is NP-hard, the BTD technique uses some approximations (described in [JT03]). We note here that Toulbar2 is designed for solving optimization problems, namely weighted CSPs, or WCSPs. In a WCSP instance, certain partial assignments have an associated cost. However, the Toulbar2 solver can be used to solve standard CSPs by simply setting all costs to 0.

For all of the results, the times given are elapsed times on a Lenovo 3000 N200 laptop with an Intel Core 2 Duo processor running at 1.66 GHz with 2 GB of RAM. Each generated instance was run five times and the mean times and mean number of restarts are shown[5].

For our experiments we used similar instances to the ones described in Section 3.6. However, this time we generated one more group in order to make the instances unsatisfiable. For clarity, we present those instances again here.

Example 5.22 *We consider a family of instances specified by two parameters, w and d. They have $((d-1) * w + 2) * w$ variables arranged in groups of size w, each with domain $\{0, \ldots, d-1\}$. We impose a constraint of arity $2w$ on each pair of successive groups, requiring that the sum of the values assigned to the first of these two groups should be strictly smaller than the sum of the values assigned to the second. This ensures that the instances generated are unsatisfiable. An instance with $w = 2$ and $d = 2$ is shown diagrammatically and defined using the specification language MiniZinc [NSB+07] in Figures 5.1(a) and 5.1(b) respectively[6]. A similar*

---

[5]MiniSAT and simple-MiniSAT were run with different seeds for each of the five runs of an instance. Instances marked with * were run once only. The runtime of simple-MiniSAT on those instances exceeded 6 h. Moreover, Toulbar2 was run with parameter $B = 1$ which enables BTD.

[6]In order to run an instance on a CSP-solver one must usually use a translator to convert the original model. The MiniZinc distribution provides an mzn2fzn translator, while for Minion one can use Tailor [GMR08].

(a)

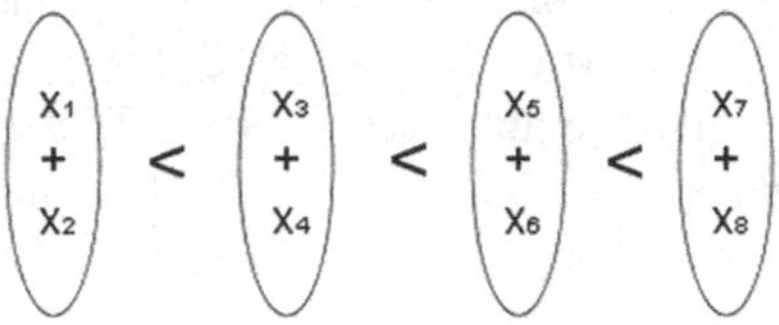

Graphical representation.

(b)

array[1..4] of var 0..1 : $X1$;
array[1..4] of var 0..1 : $X2$;
constraint
forall(i in 1..3)(
$X1[i] + X2[i] < X1[i+1] + X2[i+1]$);
solve satisfy;

Specification in MiniZinc.

(c)
$x1$ 0 1
$x2$ 0 1
$x3$ 0 1
$x4$ 0 1
$x5$ 0 1
$x6$ 0 1
$x7$ 0 1
$x8$ 0 1
hard($x1 + x2 < x3 + x4$)
hard($x3 + x4 < x5 + x6$)
hard($x5 + x6 < x7 + x8$)

Specification in *cp* format.

Fig. 5.1 An example of a CSP instance with $w = 2$, $d = 2$ and tree-width $= 3$.

format is used for Toulbar2 [7] *and the same instance encoded in this format is shown in Figure 5.1(c) (note that each hard constraint has cost 0).*

The structure of the instances described in Example 5.22 has a simple tree-decomposition as a path of nodes, with each node corresponding to a constraint scope. Hence the tree-width of these instances is $2w - 1$ and they can be shown to be unsatisfiable by enforcing $(2w - 1)$-consistency [ABD07]. However, these instances cannot be solved efficiently using standard propagation algorithms which only prune individual domain values.

The structure of the direct encoding of these instances also has a tree-decomposition with each node corresponding to a constraint scope in the original CSP instance. However, because the direct encoding introduces d Boolean variables to represent each variable in the original instance, the tree-width of the encoded SAT instances is larger by approximately a factor of d; it is in fact $2wd - 1$ (see Figure 5.2).

Table 5.1 shows the runtimes of simple-MiniSAT and the original MiniSAT solver on this family of instances, along with times for the two state-of-the-art CSP-solvers and the WCSP-solver Toulbar2. By far the best solver for this set of instances is Toulbar2, which is explicitly designed to exploit low tree-width by constructing

---

[7] A cp2wcsp translator and a description of the *cp* and *wcsp* formats is available at http://carlit.toulouse.inra.fr/cgi-bin/awki.cgi/SoftCSP.

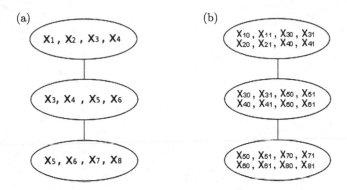

(a)   (b)

Tree-decomposition of the original   Tree-decomposition of its direct
instance.   encoding.

Fig. 5.2 Tree-decompositions of the CSP instance from Figure 5.1.

Table 5.1 Average performance of solvers on instances from Example 5.22.

group size (w)	domain size (d)	CSP variables (n)	Minion (s)	G12 (s)	Toulbar2 (s)	MiniSAT (s)	simple-MiniSAT (s)	simple-MiniSAT restarts
2	2	8	0.055	0.010	0.021	0.003	0.002	19
2	3	12	0.053	0.011	0.023	0.005	0.007	157
2	4	16	0.057	0.013	0.040	0.015	0.034	820
2	5	20	0.084	0.047	0.091	0.043	0.188	3 039
2	6	24	1.048	0.959	0.199	0.126	0.789	7 797
2	7	28	47.295	122.468	0.549	0.362	2.884	17 599
2	8	32	> 20 min	> 20 min	1.214	0.895	9.878	36 108
2	9	36	> 20 min	> 20 min	2.523	2.407	34.352	65 318
2	10	40	> 20 min	> 20 min	4.930	5.656	111.912	114 827
3	2	15	0.055	0.010	0.024	0.004	0.008	167
3	3	24	0.412	0.034	0.103	0.066	0.503	5 039
3	4	33	> 20 min	7.147	0.860	1.334	20.054	41 478
3	5	42	> 20 min	> 20 min	5.646	20.984	817.779	210 298
3	6	51	> 20 min	> 20 min	28.663	383.564	> 20 min	731 860
4	2	24	0.060	0.015	0.046	0.012	0.118	1 617
4	3	40	> 20 min	11.523	1.246	4.631	260.656	108 113
4	4	56	> 20 min	> 20 min	20.700	1,160.873	> 20 min	1 322 784*

a tree-decomposition. For the class of instances we are considering, the widths of the tree-decompositions found by Toulbar2 matched the tree-widths of the instances tested (i.e., $2w - 1$).

However, we also note that MiniSAT is remarkably effective in solving these chains of inequalities, compared to Minion and G12, even though the use of

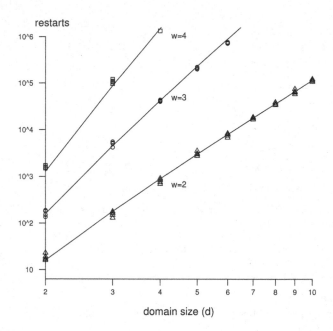

Fig. 5.3 Log-log plot of the number of restarts/conflicts used by simple-MiniSAT on the instances from Example 5.22. The solid lines show a growth function of $d^{2w-2}\binom{nd/w}{3}$, where n is the number of CSP variables. This empirically derived polynomial function appears to fit the experimental data well, and is much lower than the upper bound on the expected number of restarts calculated in Theorem 5.20 which is $O(d^{4w-2}n^{4w-2})$.

MiniSAT requires encoding each instance into a large number of clauses with a much larger tree-width than the original. Although our simplified version of the MiniSAT solver takes a little longer than the current highly optimised version, it still performs very well on these instances in comparison with the conventional CSP-solvers. Moreover, the number of restarts (and hence the number of conflicts) appears to grow only polynomially with the size of the instance (see Figure 5.3). In all cases the actual number of restarts is much lower than the polynomial upper bound on the expected number of restarts given in Theorem 5.20. We note here, however, that we used the constraint solvers as "black-boxes". Perhaps if we set a specific search strategy or simply used a different model, for example, introduced an auxiliary variable for each sum, G12 and Minion could have solved the instances of the chains of inequalities family efficiently.

Our best theoretical upper bounds on the expected run-time were obtained for the Decision learning scheme (Theorem 5.20), but the standard version of MiniSAT uses the 1UIP learning scheme with *conflict clause minimization*. To allow a direct comparison with these theoretical upper bounds, we implemented the Decision scheme in simple-MiniSAT. As the 1UIP learning scheme has generally been found to be more efficient in practice [ZMMM01], we switched off conflict clause minimization in simple-MiniSAT in order to compare the two standard learning

Table 5.2 Average performance of simple-MiniSAT with the 1UIP and the Decision learning schemes on instances from Example 5.22.

group size (w)	domain size (d)	CSP variables (n)	no. of clauses in the direct encoding	simple-MiniSAT 1UIP (s)	simple-MiniSAT 1UIP restarts	simple-MiniSAT Decision (s)	simple-MiniSAT Decision restarts
2	2	8	49	0.002	21	0.002	23
2	3	12	298	0.008	203	0.010	267
2	4	16	1 162	0.048	1 026	0.057	1 424
2	5	20	3 415	0.272	4 068	0.323	5 283
2	6	24	8 315	1.399	12 029	1.526	14 104
2	7	28	17 724	5.780	27 356	6.035	33 621
2	8	32	34 228	24.417	56 193	20.436	64 262
2	9	36	61 257	95.278	109 862	69.144	113 460
2	10	40	103 205	309.980	199 399	207.342	190 063
3	2	15	198	0.009	192	0.012	287
3	3	24	3 141	0.643	5 952	0.750	7 308
3	4	33	23 611	53.067	63 952	71.778	91 283
3	5	42	113 406	2,266.627	375 849	2,036.456	391,664
3	6	51	408 720	> 6 h	1 584 012*	> 6 h	1 365 481*
4	2	24	863	0.141	1 937	0.192	2 592
4	3	40	34 666	603.241	155 842	938.836	253 153

schemes and ran a further set of experiments. We counted the number of restarts for these two modified solvers on instances of the form described in Example 5.22 — see Table 5.2.

Note that although the performance of simple-MiniSAT with the Decision learning scheme and the 1UIP scheme are significantly worse than the performance of the original simple-MiniSAT solver, only about twice as many restarts were required for each instance. Hence, our theoretical upper bounds are still easily met for both of these standard learning schemes.

5.6 Summary

We have shown that the notion of k-consistency can be precisely captured by a single inference rule on the direct encoding of a CSP instance, restricted to deriving only clauses with at most k literals. We used this to show that a clause-learning SAT-solver with a purely random branching strategy will simulate the effect of enforcing k-consistency in expected polynomial-time, for all fixed k. This is sufficient to ensure that such solvers are able to solve certain problem families much more efficiently than conventional CSP-solvers relying on GAC-propagation.

In principle, clause-learning SAT-solvers can also do much more. It is known that, with an appropriate branching strategy and restart policy, they are able to polynomially simulate (p-simulate) general resolution [BKS04, PD09], and general resolution proofs can be exponentially shorter than the negative-hyper-resolution proofs we have considered here [HM05]. In practice, it seems that current clause-learning SAT-solvers with highly tuned learning schemes, branching strategies and restart policies are often able to exploit structure in the Boolean encoding of a CSP instance even more effectively than local consistency techniques. Hence considerable work remains to be done in understanding the relevant features of instances which they are able to exploit, in order to predict their effectiveness in solving different kinds of CSP instances.

Chapter 6
From CSP to SAT: language restrictions

The simplest explanation is always the most likely.
Agatha Christie

In CSP-solver competitions [vDLR09, vDLR08] in the last few years one SAT-based constraint solver, called Sugar [TTKB09], was exceptionally efficient and even won in a few categories. Surprisingly, it outperformed standard constraint solvers on many instances involving global constraints, which are supposed to be a particular strength of CSP-solvers.

The SAT encoding that the Sugar solver implements is called the *order encoding*. In this chapter we show that this encoding, unlike other common encodings, transforms instances of various tractable language classes of the constraint satisfaction problem into easily recognised tractable instances of SAT. We also show that such instances will then be solved by standard SAT-solvers in linear time.

6.1 Tractable CSP languages

In this section we start by describing the six tractable language classes for SAT. Several of these can be generalised and correspond to some tractable CSP languages introduced in Chapter 3, examples of which we present in the rest of this section.

6.1.1 The Boolean case: tractable languages for SAT

To study possible language restrictions for SAT, we consider subproblems of the form SAT(Φ), where Φ is a set of relations over the Boolean domain, and SAT(Φ) consists of all SAT instances whose constraint relations belong to Φ. Schaefer's

© Springer International Publishing Switzerland 2015
J. Petke, *Bridging Constraint Satisfaction and Boolean Satisfiability*,
Artificial Intelligence: Foundations, Theory, and Algorithms,
DOI 10.1007/978-3-319-21810-6_6

well-known dichotomy theorem [Sch78] identifies all the tractable languages for SAT:

Theorem 6.1 ([Sch78]) *Let Φ be a finite set of Boolean relations. If Φ satisfies at least one of the conditions below then SAT(Φ) is tractable. Otherwise SAT(Φ) is NP-complete.*

1. *Every relation in Φ evaluates to true if all arguments are true.*
2. *Every relation in Φ evaluates to true if all arguments are false.*
3. *Every relation in Φ can be expressed as a Horn formula.*
4. *Every relation in Φ can be expressed as a dual-Horn formula.*
5. *Every relation in Φ can be expressed as a 2CNF formula.*
6. *Every relation in Φ can be expressed as an affine formula.*

A formula is called *Horn* if it is a conjunction of clauses where every clause contains at most one positive literal. It is *dual-Horn*, if it is a conjunction of clauses where every clause has at most one negative literal. A *2CNF formula* is a conjunction of clauses containing at most two literals each, and an *affine formula* is a conjunction of linear equations over the two-element field.

6.1.2 A trivial case: Constant-closed constraints

A CSP instance is *constant-closed* if every constraint in it allows the constant value d to be assigned to all variables in its scope, for some fixed d. Such instances are trivially tractable, because they can be solved by the trivial linear algorithm that assigns the value d to every variable in the instance.

6.1.3 Max-closed constraints

A rather more interesting family of tractable constraint satisfaction problems is the class of CSPs whose constraints are all *max-closed*, as defined in Definition 3.2.

Max-closed constraints can take many forms, as shown in Section 3.3. For example, all unary constraints on any totally ordered domain are max-closed, and certain non-linear numerical constraints, such as $6v_1v_3v_5 \geq 3v_2+2$ are max-closed. They all can be solved by a polynomial-time algorithm that enforces generalised-arc-consistency [CJ06].

Theorem 6.2 *A CSP instance that contains only max-closed constraints can be solved by enforcing generalised-arc-consistency.*

Proof Let P be a CSP instance that contains only max-closed constraints. After enforcing generalised-arc-consistency on P a value d is in the domain of variable v if and only if for every constraint C in P there exists a tuple t satisfying C such that $t[v] = d$. If the domain of any variable is empty, then the instance is unsatisfiable and we are done. Otherwise, let $max(v)$ be the maximum domain value in the generalised-arc-consistent domain of some variable v. We claim that the tuple $t = (v_1 = max(v_1), v_2 = max(v_2), \ldots, v_n = max(v_n))$ solves P. Assume, for contradiction, that t is not a solution for P. Then there exists some constraint $C \in P$ that disallows t. Because all the variable domains are generalised-arc-consistent, for each variable $v_i \in C$ there exists a satisfying tuple t_i such that $t_i[v_i] = max(v_i)$. Applying the max operator to all such tuples produces the tuple t' such that $t'[v_i] = max(v_i)$ for all $v_i \in C$. As C is still max-closed after enforcing generalised-arc-consistency, t' satisfies C. As $variables(t') = variables(C)$ and $t' \subseteq t$, t satisfies C and we reach a contradiction. Hence, the satisfiability of a max-closed CSP instance P can be established by enforcing generalised-arc-consistency. □

Since generalised-arc-consistency can be achieved in polynomial-time [Bes06], the next result follows.

Corollary 6.3 *A CSP instance that contains only max-closed constraints can be solved in $O(erd^r)$ time, where e is the number of constraints, d is the domain size and r is the greatest arity among all constraints.*

6.1.4   Connected-row-convex constraints

Connected-row-convex constraints were defined in Section 3.5 using a standard matrix representation of binary relations.

It has been known for some time that the class of connected-row-convex constraints can be solved in polynomial-time by an algorithm that enforces *path-consistency* (see Definition 2.12). Recently this result has been strengthened by considering another type of consistency known as *singleton arc-consistency* (see Definition 2.16).

Theorem 6.4 *A CSP instance that contains only connected-row-convex constraints can be solved by enforcing singleton arc-consistency.*

Proof All connected-row-convex relations have a majority polymorphism [CJ06]. Hence, they can be solved by a singleton arc-consistency algorithm, by Theorem 26 in [CDG11]. □

By using the complexity result from [CDG11] we get the following result:

Corollary 6.5 *A CSP instance that contains only connected-row-convex constraints can be solved in $O(end^3)$ time, where e is the number of constraints, d is the domain size and n is the number of variables.*

6.2   Standard SAT encodings

In Chapter 4 we presented various SAT encodings of CSP instances which have been proposed throughout the years. We concentrated on the most general encodings that represent all constraints in the same manner, regardless of their type. This can be achieved, as every finite constraint relation can be represented by a set of tuples it supports or disallows. In this section we will show that the way the domains are encoded into SAT has a huge impact on the complexity of the resultant SAT instance.

Proposition 6.6 *No sparse encoding of a CSP instance with domain size* > 2 *belongs to a tractable language class of SAT.*

Proof Let v be a CSP variable with domain $\{1, 2, \ldots, d\}$. A sparse encoding (see Section 4.1) introduces d Boolean variables, $\{x_{v1}, x_{v2}, \cdots, x_{vd}\}$, to represent possible assignments to v. The encoding must also include a suitable set of clauses to enforce the "exactly-one" constraint on these variables, as in any solution of the CSP instance exactly one of the x_{vi} must be assigned *True*.

   However, the exactly-one relation on $d > 2$ Boolean variables does not lie in any of the 6 tractable language classes for SAT [Sch78]. Hence the clauses which encode the exactly-one relation do not all fall into any one of these tractable language classes.   □

Proposition 6.7 *The log encoding of any CSP instance with domain size* > 4 *containing certain unary constraints does not belong to any tractable language class of SAT.*

Proof Let $\{x_{[1]}, \cdots, x_{[r]}\}$ be the Boolean variables representing a CSP variable v under the log encoding (see Section 4.2) of some instance P. Assume P contains unary constraints that restrict v to values that are a power of 2. The clauses representing these constraints must allow precisely those assignments where exactly one of the $x_{[i]}$s is true. Hence the log encoding of P must enforce the exactly-one constraint on $\{x_{[1]}, \ldots, x_{[r]}\}$. If the size of the domain of v is greater than 4, then $r > 2$ and the exactly-one constraint does not fall into any of the six tractable language classes for SAT [Sch78]. Hence the clauses which encode this unary constraint do not all fall into any one of these tractable language classes.   □

6.3   The order encoding

All of the SAT encodings considered in the previous section use one or more Boolean variables to represent each possible assignment of a CSP variable, $v = i$. As mentioned in Section 4.3, there is also another possibility of representing CSP domains, that is to use *regular variables*. The authors of the *order encoding* took this approach [TTKB09].

Let P be a CSP instance containing a variable v with domain $\{1, 2, \ldots, d\}$. Its order encoding, F, will contain the following set of Boolean variables to represent v: $\{x_{v1}^{\leq}, x_{v2}^{\leq}, \cdots, x_{v(d-1)}^{\leq}\}$, where each $x_{vi}^{\leq}$ represents the comparison $v \leq i$. Moreover, F will contain clauses $\neg x_{v(i-1)}^{\leq} \vee x_{vi}^{\leq}$, for $i = 2, 3, \ldots, d-1$, to ensure that these variables are consistently assigned.

Finally, clauses are added to represent the constraints, to rule out any assignment to the Boolean variables that violates a constraint. For example, if a unary constraint on variable v excludes the value i from its domain, then we add the clause $\neg x_{vi}^{\leq} \vee x_{v(i-1)}^{\leq}$, to represent the constraint that $(v > i) \vee (v \leq i - 1)$. Note that an arbitrary unary constraint on a finite domain can be represented as a conjunction of such binary clauses.

Definition 6.8 ([TTKB09]) *Let $P = (V, D, C)$ be a CSP instance, in which D is the set $\{1, 2, \ldots, d\}$, and assume that every constraint of P is of the form $\sum_{i=1}^{n} a_i v_i \leq c$, where a_is are non-zero integer constants, c is an integer constant, and the v_is are mutually distinct integer variables[1].*

The order encoding *of P, taking values in D, will be a conjunction of the following clauses, where each inequality of the form $v \leq j$ is represented by a Boolean variable, $x_{vj}^{\leq}$:*

- *for all $v_i \in V$ and $j \in D$ such that $2 \leq j \leq d-1$: $\neg(v_i \leq j-1) \vee (v_i \leq j)$*
- *for all constraints $\sum_{i=1}^{n} a_i v_i \leq c$:*

$$\bigwedge_{(b_1,\ldots,b_n) \in B} \bigvee_i \begin{cases} v_i \leq \lfloor \frac{b_i}{a_i} \rfloor & (a_i > 0) \\ \neg(v_i \leq \lceil \frac{b_i}{a_i} \rceil - 1) & (a_i < 0) \end{cases}$$

where B is the set of integer tuples defined by

$$\left\{ (b_1, \ldots, b_n) \mid \sum_{i=1}^{n} b_i = c - n + 1, \bigwedge_{i=1}^{n} min(a_i v_i) - 1 \leq b_i \leq max(a_i v_i) \right\}$$

It turns out that under the order encoding, unlike the encodings considered earlier, certain tractable CSP classes are translated to tractable language classes of SAT.

Theorem 6.9 *If a CSP instance $P = (V, D, C)$ is constant-closed under the lowest or the highest domain value, then its order encoding will also be constant-closed.*

Proof Let $P = (V, D, C)$ be a CSP instance defined on domain $D = \{1, \ldots, d\}$. If P allows value 1 to be assigned to every variable $v \in V$, its order encoding will be satisfied by assigning the value *True* to all the Boolean variables $x_{vi}^{\leq}$. On the other hand, if P allows value d to be assigned to every variable $v \in V$, its order encoding

---

[1] Other types of constraints can be translated into SAT using the order encoding by first expressing them in terms of inequalities as shown in Figure 2 in [TTKB09].

will be satisfied by assigning the value *False* to all the Boolean variables $x_{vi}^{\leq}$. Hence, the result follows.   □

A similar result can be obtained for max-closed constraints, thanks to the following theorem and corollary:

Theorem 6.10 ([JC95]) *A constraint over an ordered domain is max-closed if and only if it is logically equivalent to a conjunction of disjunctions of the following form:*

$$(v_i < e_i) \vee (v_1 > d_1) \vee \cdots \vee (v_n > d_n).$$

where each v_i is a variable (not necessarily distinct), and the e_i, d_i are domain values.

Corollary 6.11 ([JC95]) *If the domain of the variables is $\{True, False\}$, with False $<$ True, then a constraint is min-closed if and only if it is logically equivalent to a conjunction of Horn clauses.*

Theorem 6.12 *If a CSP instance P contains only max-closed constraints, then its order encoding will be min-closed.*

Proof By Theorem 6.10, every max-closed constraint can be represented as a set of constraints of the form $(v_i < e_i) \vee (v_1 > d_1) \vee \cdots \vee (v_n > d_n)$. Hence, the order encoding of a max-closed CSP instance P will produce the following set of clauses:

- for all $v_i \in V$ and $d_i \in D$ such that $2 \leq d_i \leq d - 1$: $\neg(v_i \leq d_i - 1) \vee (v_i \leq d_i)$
- for all constraints $(v_i < e_i) \vee (v_1 > d_1) \vee \cdots \vee (v_n > d_n)$:
$$(v_i \leq e_i - 1) \vee \neg(v_1 \leq d_1) \vee \cdots \vee \neg(v_n \leq d_n).$$

As each inequality of the form $v \leq d_i$ is represented by a Boolean variable, $x_{vd_i}^{\leq}$, we end up with a set of Horn clauses, which are min-closed by Corollary 6.11.   □

Note that if we directly translate a set of max-closed inequalities into SAT using the order encoding, we also end up with a Horn formula. For all constraints $\sum_{i=1}^{n}(a_i x_i) \leq c$ the following clauses are produced:

$$\bigwedge_{\sum_{i=1}^{n-1}(b_i = c - n + 1)} (\bigvee_i \neg(x_i \leq \lceil \frac{b_i}{a_i} \rceil - 1) \vee x_n \leq \lfloor \frac{b_n}{a_n} \rfloor)$$

where b_i's range over integers satisfying $\sum_{i=1}^{n} b_i = c - n + 1$ and $min(a_i x_i) - 1 \leq b_i \leq max(a_i x_i)$ for all i and non-zero a_i.

A similar result can be obtained for connected-row-convex constraints, thanks to the following theorem, which shows that they have a very simple representation in terms of disjunctions of inequalities.

Theorem 6.13 ([CJJK00]) *A constraint over an ordered domain is connected-row-convex if and only if it is logically equivalent to a conjunction of disjunctions of the following forms:*

$$v \leq d_i \vee w \leq d_j$$
$$v \leq d_i \vee w \geq d_j$$
$$v \geq d_i \vee w \leq d_j \qquad\qquad (6.1)$$
$$v \geq d_i \vee w \geq d_j.$$

where v and w are variables (not necessarily distinct), and d_i, d_j are domain values.

Corollary 6.14 *If the domain of the variables is {True, False}, then a constraint is connected-row-convex if and only if it is logically equivalent to a conjunction of 2CNF clauses over literals representing comparisons.*

Theorem 6.15 *If a CSP instance P contains only connected-row-convex constraints, then its order encoding will also be connected-row-convex.*

Proof By Theorem 6.13, each connected-row-convex constraint can be represented as a set of disjunctions of inequalities of the form (6.1). The order encoding of a CSP instance P that contains such constraints will produce the following clauses:

- for all $v_i \in V$ and $d_i \in D$ such that $2 \leq d_i \leq d - 1$: $\neg(v_i \leq d_i - 1) \vee (v_i \leq d_i)$
- for all constraints C:

$$
\begin{array}{lll}
v_i \leq d_i \vee v_j \leq d_j & \text{if} & C = v_i \leq d_i \vee v_j \leq d_j \\
v_i \leq d_i \vee \neg(v_j \leq d_j - 1) & \text{if} & C = v_i \leq d_i \vee v_j \geq d_j \\
\neg(v_i \leq d_i - 1) \vee v_j \leq d_j & \text{if} & C = v_i \geq d_i \vee v_j \leq d_j \\
\neg(v_i \leq d_i - 1) \vee \neg(v_j \leq d_j - 1) & \text{if} & C = v_i \geq d_i \vee v_j \geq d_j
\end{array}
\qquad (6.2)
$$

As each inequality of the form $v \leq d_i$ is represented by a Boolean variable, we end up with a set of binary clauses, which are connected-row-convex by Corollary 6.14. $\qquad\square$

6.4   Full regular encodings

We note that a sparse encoding introduces a Boolean variable x_{vi} representing each assignment $v = i$, but the order encoding introduces a Boolean variable $x_{vi}^{\leq}$ representing each comparison $v \leq i$. In this section, we will consider another suggested type of encoding that uses a similar idea to the order encoding.

Proposition 6.16 *The full regular direct encoding of any CSP instance P with non-unary constraints belongs to a tractable language class of SAT if and only if the constraints of P are constant-closed under the highest or lowest domain value. The same applies to the full regular (minimal) support encoding.*

Proof Let $\bigvee(\neg x_{vi})$ be a conflict clause in the direct encoding of some non-unary constraint. Under the full regular direct encoding such a clause is translated into the following formula: $\bigvee(x^{\geq}_{v(i+1)} \vee \neg x^{\geq}_{vi})$, which does not belong to any tractable language class of SAT, except the constant-closed classes.

Let $\neg x_{vj} \vee \bigvee x_{wi}$ be a support clause in the support encoding of some non-unary constraint. Under the full regular support encoding such a clause is translated into a conjunction of clauses of the form $(x^{\geq}_{v(j+1)} \vee \neg x^{\geq}_{vj} \vee x^{\geq}_{w(i+1)}) \wedge (x^{\geq}_{v(j+1)} \vee \neg x^{\geq}_{vj} \vee \neg x^{\geq}_{wi})$, which does not belong to any tractable language class of SAT except the constant-closed classes.

If a CSP instance is closed under the highest or lowest domain value, a full regular direct encoding of such an instance will be constant-closed for the value *False* or *True*, respectively, but in all other cases there will be a constraint which is violated by assigning all variables the highest value, and a constraint which is violated by assigning all variables the lowest value. These constraints must be represented by clauses which are not all members of either of the constant-closed classes.   □

6.5   Performance of DPLL-based SAT-solvers on tractable CSPs

It has been shown experimentally in [TTKB09] that the order encoding gives better solver performance compared with the direct and support encodings on instances of the graph colouring and open-shop scheduling problems. Our theoretical results above suggest that the order encoding will also be a better choice of encoding than a sparse or log encoding for all CSP instances over the tractable constraint languages we have considered. In this section we investigate to what extent this is true in practice with a current SAT-solver.

Throughout this section when we refer to a clause-learning SAT-solver we mean a *Conflict-Driven Clause Learning* SAT-solver that implements the *DPLL* algorithm and an *asserting learning scheme*, as defined in Chapter 4 of [Pre09].

We generated various instances of the three tractable CSP classes discussed in this chapter. All the instances generated are specified by 3 parameters: the number of variables, the maximum domain value, and the number of constraints. The domain for every variable in our instances is $1 \ldots d$, where d is the maximum domain value.

All the instances generated were then encoded using the direct, log and order encodings. For the order encoding we used Sugar's built-in CSP-to-SAT translator, but without the optimizations described in [TTKB09] that introduce new variables. For the other encodings we wrote custom translators.

We ran all the encoded instances on the state-of-the-art clause-learning SAT-solver, MiniSAT [ES03] version 2-070721. For all of the results, the times given are elapsed times on a Lenovo 3000 N200 laptop with an Intel Core 2 Duo processor running at 1.66 GHz with 2 GB of RAM. For each set of parameters we generated four instances and report the average timings.

```
(int v1 1 5)
(int v2 1 5)
(int v3 1 5)
(<= -7 (+ (mul 5 v1) (mul -7 v3) ) )
(<= -12 (+ (mul 10 v1) (mul -7 v2) (mul -10 v3) ) )
(<= -4 (+ (mul -8 v1) (mul 2 v2) (mul 4 v3) ) )
(<= 6 (+ (mul 5 v1) (mul 8 v2) (mul 2 v3) ) )
```

Fig. 6.1 A constant-closed CSP instance in *.csp* format [TTKB09] that is satisfied by the assignment ($v1 = 1, v2 = 1, v3 = 1$). For example, the fourth line of the instance represents the constraint $-7 \le 5v_1 - 7v_3$.

6.5.1   Constant-closed constraints

Proposition 6.17 *If a CSP instance P allows the lowest (or highest) domain value to be assigned to all its variables, then a DPLL-based SAT-solver with an appropriate value order will decide the satisfiability of the order encoding of P in linear time.*

Proof Each clause of the order encoding of a constant-closed constraint under the lowest domain value has at least one positive literal. Hence, a DPLL-based SAT-solver, that assigns the value *True* first to each variable, will not need to backtrack, and hence will decide its satisfiability in linear time in the size of the instance. Similarly, the satisfiability of a constant-closed instance under the highest domain value will be decided by a DPLL-based SAT-solver with the opposite value order in linear time.   □

In order to generate instances that were constant-closed under the lowest (or highest) domain value, we generated random inequalities and then selected those that satisfied the required constant solution. An example is shown in Figure 6.1.

As predicted by Theorem 6.9, for all constraints that were constant-closed under the lowest domain value, the formulae generated by the Sugar solver contained at least one positive literal in each clause. Moreover, the instances that were satisfied by assigning the highest domain value to each variable contained at least one negative literal in each clause. The runtimes of MiniSAT on these two families of instances[2] are presented in Table 6.1.

It is clear from these results that the order encoding is much better than the others for solving these kinds of instances. The order encoding usually produced fewer clauses than the other encodings for instances of this type. However, Mini-SAT's performance was still much better on the clauses produced by the order encoding even in those cases where this encoding produced a larger set of clauses than the other encodings. For instance, for parameters $(9, 3, 100)$ the direct and

---

[2]For the instances satisfied by assigning the lowest domain value to every variable, we changed the value ordering to assign True before False. In all other cases we used MiniSAT's default value ordering, which assigns False first.

Table 6.1 Performance of MiniSAT on the direct, log and order encoding of constant-closed CSP instances of the form shown in Figure 6.1

number of CSP variables	number of CSP values	number of constraints	MiniSAT (s) direct encoding	MiniSAT (s) log encoding	MiniSAT (s) order encoding
instances satisfied by assigning the lowest domain value to every variable					
3	10	100	0.01	0.07	0.00
6	6	10	22.55	489.60	0.10
9	3	10	7.52	39.90	0.08
9	3	100	7.70	39.84	1.76
9	4	10	> 20 min	> 20 min	4.64
10	3	10	130.34	837.75	0.39
instances satisfied by assigning the highest domain value to every variable					
3	10	100	0.02	0.07	0.00
6	6	10	17.90	348.19	0.06
9	3	10	6.16	28.47	0.06
9	3	100	7.60	40.60	0.90
9	4	10	> 20 min	> 20 min	5.04
10	3	10	119.39	754.83	0.61

log encodings produced around 19 700 clauses each, whereas the order encoding produced an average of 46 957 clauses.

6.5.2   Max-closed constraints

Proposition 6.18 *If a CSP instance P contains only max-closed constraints, then a DPLL-based SAT-solver which assigns False before True will decide the satisfiability of the order encoding of P in linear time.*

Proof Let F be the order encoding of P. As long as F contains a unit clause, unit propagation takes place. Next, either the solver terminates after discovering an empty clause, or a set of Horn clauses of size > 1 remain. Each such clause contains at least one negative literal. Hence, if a solver then decides to assign value *False* to each variable, every clause will be satisfied and a solution will be found. As unit propagation takes linear time [DG84, Pre09, ZM02], the result follows.   □

To obtain satisfiable CSP instances with max-closed constraints, we generated inequality constraints of the form shown below.

$$a_1 v_1 + a_2 v_2 + \cdots + a_{r-1} v_{r-1} \geq a_r v_r + c \tag{6.3}$$

We then selected only those that satisfied some fixed random solution. An example instance is shown in Figure 6.2.

Fig. 6.2 An example of a satisfiable max-closed CSP instance.

```
(int v1 1 5)
(int v2 1 5)
(int v3 1 5)
(<= 10 (+ (mul -6 v1) (mul 9 v2) (mul 4 v3) ) )
(<= -3 (+ (mul -10 v1) (mul 2 v2) (mul 4 v3) ) )
(<= 16 (+ (mul 7 v1) (mul 1 v2) (mul 10 v3) ) )
(<= -1 (+ (mul 7 v1) (mul -6 v2) (mul 6 v3) ) )
```

Table 6.2 Performance of MiniSAT on the direct, log and order encoding of max-closed CSP instances of the form shown in Figure 6.2

number of CSP variables	number of CSP values	number of constraints	MiniSAT (s) direct encoding	MiniSAT (s) log encoding	MiniSAT (s) order encoding
satisfiable instances					
3	10	100	0.01	0.06	0.00
6	6	10	7.42	95.97	0.07
9	3	10	1.30	4.99	0.01
9	3	100	5.15	23.27	0.59
9	4	10	> 20 min	> 20 min	0.73
10	3	10	20.08	107.38	0.11
unsatisfiable instances					
3	10	100	0.02	0.06	0.00
6	6	10	26.64	515.90	0.01
9	3	10	7.85	41.12	0.00
9	3	100	7.87	40.15	0.02
9	4	10	> 20 min	> 20 min	0.02
10	3	10	140.68	907.51	0.01

To generate unsatisfiable instances, we used the same technique as before and then added two further inequalities of the following form:

$$
\begin{aligned}
\left(\sum_{i \in \{1,\dots,n\} \setminus \{k\}} v_i \right) - v_k \geq d(n-1) - 1 \\
\left(\sum_{i \in \{1,\dots,n\} \setminus \{j\}} v_i \right) - v_j \geq d(n-1) - 1
\end{aligned}
\tag{6.4}
$$

for some $j \neq k$, where n is the number of variables in the instance and d is the maximum domain value.

We encoded the generated instances using the direct, log and order encodings. As predicted by Theorem 6.12, the order encodings of these max-closed instances contained Horn clauses only. The runtimes of MiniSAT on the various encodings are presented in Table 6.2.

The results show that the order encoding outperforms the other two encodings, as expected. Moreover, in the unsatisfiable case MiniSAT detects the unsatisfiability purely by unit propagation — no variable is picked for branching. Hence, it is even quicker in solving unsatisfiable instances than in solving the satisfiable ones. The opposite seems to be true for the other two encodings.

6.5.3 Connected-row-convex constraints

Proposition 6.19 *If a CSP instance P contains only connected-row-convex constraints, then a clause-learning SAT-solver will decide the satisfiability of the order encoding of P after a linear number of conflicts.*

Proof Let F be the order encoding of P. By Theorem 6.15, we know that F is in 2CNF. Consider the case when after unit propagation some binary clause C is falsified. The literals of C have been assigned at the current decision level (since a previous assignment of one of its literals would cause the clause to be either satisfied or become unit and hence trigger further unit propagation). Each clause that caused literals of C to be assigned will also contain literals that have been assigned at the current decision level. As an asserting learning scheme adds a clause that contains only one variable that has been assigned at the current decision level, it will backtrack to a unit clause and add its negation to the clause set. As at most n unit clauses can be added, where n is the number of variables in P, a clause-learning SAT-solver will terminate after at most n conflicts.   ☐

We wrote a program to generate instances of the form shown in Equation 6.1. For the satisfiable case we ensured that each constraint in an instance satisfied some fixed random solution. For the unsatisfiable case we added four constraints imposed on two randomly picked variables of the form in Equation 6.5.

$$
\begin{aligned}
v_i &\leq a \vee v_j \leq b \\
v_i &\geq a + 1 \vee v_j \leq b \\
v_i &\leq a \vee v_j \geq b + 1 \\
v_i &\geq a + 1 \vee v_j \geq b + 1
\end{aligned}
\tag{6.5}
$$

An example instance is shown in Figure 6.3.

Fig. 6.3 An example of an unsatisfiable connected-row-convex CSP instance. The last four constraints ensure that the instance is trivially unsatisfiable.

```
(int v1 1 5)
(int v2 1 5)
(int v3 1 5)
(or (<= v1 1) (<= v2 4) )
(or (<= v2 2) (>= v3 3) )
(or (>= v3 3) (>= v1 1) )
(or (<= v3 1) (<= v2 2) )
(or (>= v3 2) (<= v2 2) )
(or (<= v3 1) (>= v2 3) )
(or (>= v3 2) (>= v2 3) )
```

Table 6.3 Performance of MiniSAT on the direct, log and order encoding of connected-row-convex CSP instances of the form shown in Figure 6.3

number of CSP variables	number of CSP values	number of constraints	MiniSAT (s) direct encoding	MiniSAT (s) log encoding	MiniSAT (s) order encoding
satisfiable instances					
100	10	100	0.01	0.01	0.00
10	100	10	0.31	6.14	0.00
100	100	10	2.85	11.76	0.02
10	100	100	15.74	645.36	0.00
10	110	100	15.75	696.07	0.00
10	200	100	226.75	> 20 min	0.00
unsatisfiable instances					
100	10	100	0.01	0.02	0.00
10	100	10	0.83	14.97	0.00
100	100	10	3.21	16.67	0.01
10	100	100	5.78	368.79	0.01
10	110	100	9.72	> 20 min	0.01
10	200	100	83.33	> 20 min	0.00

As predicted by Theorem 6.15, the order encoding of such instances produced binary clauses only. Comparison with the direct and log encoding is shown in Table 6.3.

All three encodings performed fairly well on the connected-row-convex class, although the log encoding seems to be significantly worse than the others. Since the constraints are all binary, the direct encoding actually generates a set of 2CNF clauses together with at-least-one clauses, which grow with domain size.

6.6 Summary

In this chapter we gave a theory-based argument to prefer the order encoding for certain families of constraint satisfaction problems. In particular, we showed that translating such instances using a sparse encoding or the log encoding results in SAT instances which do not fall into known tractable classes. However, translating such instances using the order encoding results in SAT instances that do fall into known tractable classes. Moreover, standard SAT-solvers will then solve them efficiently. We also provided experimental evidence that, as predicted, the order encoding is a considerably better choice in practice, with current SAT-solvers, for max-closed, connected-row-convex and certain constant-closed CSP classes than either the direct encoding or the log encoding.

We have shown that using the order encoding to translate a CSP instance that is constant-closed for the lowest domain value gives a set of clauses satisfying the first condition of Schaefer's Dichotomy Theorem. Similarly, constraints that are constant-closed under the highest domain value translate under the order encoding to clauses that satisfy the second condition of the theorem. Max-closed constraints translate to clauses satisfying the third condition of the theorem. By symmetry between min-closed and max-closed constraints, min-closed constraints translate to clauses satisfying the fourth condition of the theorem. Connected-row-convex constraints translate to clauses satisfying the fifth condition. The final, sixth, condition in Schaefer's Theorem can never be satisfied using the order encoding, since (for all domains with 3 or more elements) it is already broken by the consistency clauses, $\neg x_{vc-1}^{\leq} \vee x_{vc}^{\leq}$. Hence we have given a complete list of all constraint types which are encoded to tractable language classes for SAT using the order encoding.

It would be interesting to see if other encodings could be developed which would allow other tractable CSP languages, like linear equations, to be translated to tractable languages for SAT, and hence solved efficiently by SAT-based solvers.

Chapter 7
SAT encodings of a classical problem: a case study

"Cat among the pigeons"

Book by Agatha Christie

One of the simplest combinatorial principles in proof complexity is the pigeonhole principle. It is attributed to Dirichlet in 1834 and has been extensively studied ever since in counting arguments. The principle roughly states that if n objects are distributed over m pigeonholes where $m < n$, then at least one pigeonhole must contain more than one item. Surprisingly enough the most basic SAT encoding of the principle is not solved efficiently by SAT-solvers. One reason is that this encoding has a resolution proof of exponential size.

Various other encodings of the pigeonhole principle have been introduced. These include Cook's translation which uses non-assignment variables [Coo76]. Cook showed that his encoding allowed for an *extended* resolution proof of polynomial size[1].

In this chapter we consider this encoding and other encodings of the pigeonhole principle that have been proposed throughout the years. We give theoretical reasons why SAT-solvers are likely *not* to solve them efficiently. We will also show certain significant similarities between various encodings.

7.1   SAT encodings of the pigeonhole principle

There are many variants of the pigeonhole problem. However, here we consider one particular formulation of the problem, which states that you cannot put n pigeons into $n-1$ holes. In other words, *all* pigeons must be in *different* holes. This problem has a very simple CSP model: the pigeons are represented as variables with domains $\{1, \cdots, n-1\}$ with one all-different constraint imposed on all these variables.

The simplest SAT encoding of the pigeonhole principle is the multivalued direct encoding (see Section 4.1). We will call it the *standard encoding*. It translates the

---

[1]Resolution proofs of formulae that introduce new variables are called extended resolution proofs.

© Springer International Publishing Switzerland 2015
J. Petke, *Bridging Constraint Satisfaction and Boolean Satisfiability*,
Artificial Intelligence: Foundations, Theory, and Algorithms,
DOI 10.1007/978-3-319-21810-6_7

binary constraints specifying that, for all $i \neq k$, pigeon i must be assigned to a different hole than pigeon k (i.e. $p_i \neq p_k$).

Example 7.1 *The standard encoding of the pigeonhole principle introduces the following clauses:*

$$\text{domain clauses:}$$
$$p_{i1} \vee \cdots \vee p_{i(n-1)} \quad \text{for all } 1 \leq i \leq n$$

$$\text{constraint clauses:}$$
$$\neg p_{ij} \vee \neg p_{kj} \quad \text{for all } 1 \leq i < k \leq n \text{ and } 1 \leq j \leq n-1$$

Each p_{ij} denotes an assignment of pigeon i to hole j.

Example 7.2 *The pigeonhole principle can also be encoded into clauses of size 3 by introducing non-assignment variables to split the long domain clauses. In this encoding for every pigeon i a set of clauses $\neg q_{i0} \wedge (q_{i0} \vee p_{i1} \vee \neg q_{i1}) \wedge \cdots \wedge (q_{i(n-2)} \vee p_{i(n-1)} \vee \neg q_{i(n-1)}) \wedge q_{i(n-1)}$ is introduced.*

Note that the two encodings described above essentially encode the two constraints:

- each pigeon must be placed in *at least one* hole;
- *at most one* pigeon must be placed in each hole.

Another possible way of encoding the problem is to use *regular variables* representing a comparison $p_i \geq j$ each. One such encoding is the *regular encoding* which was presented in Section 4.3. It is particularly interesting as it was shown to improve solver performance when used for translating the all-different constraint [GN04], which can be used to formulate the pigeonhole principle. The regular encoding of the pigeonhole principle translates the usual at-least-one and at-most-one conditions as follows (also see Example 4.11).

Example 7.3 *The regular encoding of the pigeonhole principle produces the following set of clauses, for all $1 \leq i \leq n-1$ and $1 \leq j \leq n-2$:*

$$\text{at-least-one constraint:}$$
$$\neg p_{i2}^{\geq} \rightarrow p_{i1}$$
$$p_{ij}^{\geq} \wedge \neg p_{i(j+1)}^{\geq} \rightarrow p_{ij}$$
$$p_{i(n-1)}^{\geq} \rightarrow p_{i(n-1)}$$

$$\text{at-most-one constraint:}$$
$$p_{1j} \rightarrow \neg h_{2j}^{\geq}$$
$$p_{ij} \rightarrow h_{ij}^{\geq} \wedge \neg h_{(i+1)j}^{\geq}$$
$$p_{nj} \rightarrow h_{nj}^{\geq}$$
$$h_{(i+1)j}^{\geq} \rightarrow h_{ij}^{\geq}$$

If $p_{ij}^{\geq}$ is set to True, then pigeon i must be in a hole whose number is greater than or equal to j. If $h_{ij}^{\geq}$ is set to True, then hole j contains a pigeon whose number is at least i.

Among encodings based solely on regular variables is the *interval-based regular support encoding* (see Section 4.3). The main idea behind it is to represent with intervals the supporting values of some variable v for some other variable assignment $w = a$. The interval-based regular support encoding of the pigeonhole principle is based on the support encoding (see Section 4.1) which encodes the binary constraints $p_i \neq p_k$.

Example 7.4 *The interval-based regular support encoding of the pigeonhole principle will produce the following set of clauses, for all $1 \leq i < k \leq n$ and $1 \leq j \leq n - 2$:*

$$p_{i(j+1)}^{\geq} \rightarrow p_{ij}^{\geq}$$
$$p_{ij}^{\geq} \wedge \neg p_{i(j+1)}^{\geq} \rightarrow p_{k1}^{\geq}$$
$$p_{ij}^{\geq} \wedge \neg p_{i(j+1)}^{\geq} \wedge p_{kj}^{\geq} \rightarrow p_{k(j+1)}^{\geq}$$

As $p_{k1}^{\geq}$ is always satisfied, the second set of clauses can be omitted.

It is worth mentioning that the order encoding discussed in Section 6.3 produces essentially the same set of clauses as the interval-based regular support encoding, just with opposite signs[2].

In [FG10] experiments have been conducted on various encodings of different variants of the pigeonhole problem. Although there was no clear winner, for the problem with one pigeon per hole the *sequential counter* and *commander* encodings (see Section 4.4) were the best in terms of solving time.

It was noted in [ACLM10] that the at-most-one condition in the sequential counter encoding is the same as in the regular encoding. The commander encoding of an at-most-k constraint is presented in Example 4.13. The at-least-one condition in both encodings is translated in the same way as in the standard encoding (see Example 7.1).

7.2 Theoretical analysis

In the previous section we have identified various SAT encodings of the pigeonhole principle. Although there might be some improvements in SAT-solver performance on those encodings that introduce non-assignment variables, we will show that they do not have short extended resolution proofs (that is resolution proofs introducing

---

[2]We consider here the order encoding that contains regular variables only. We note here that in [TTKB09] auxiliary variables are allowed in the encoding to split long clauses.

non-assignment variables). From now on we will use the term "resolution proof" rather than "extended resolution proof" since each extended resolution proof of the pigeonhole principle is effectively a resolution proof of a particular CNF formula.

Firstly, observe that the extra variables in the 3CNF encoding of the pigeonhole principle can be viewed as negations of regular variables. For every pigeon i we have a set of clauses $\neg q_{i0} \wedge (q_{i0} \vee p_{i1} \vee \neg q_{i1}) \wedge \cdots \wedge (q_{i(n-2)} \vee p_{i(n-1)} \vee \neg q_{i(n-1)}) \wedge q_{i(n-1)}$. As only one of $p_{i1}, \cdots, p_{i(n-1)}$ can be satisfied, each q_{ij} can be viewed as a comparison $p_i \leq j$. Suppose we put pigeon i in hole 5. Then all p_{ij}s for $j \neq 5$ should be set to *False* (since one pigeon can be put into one hole only). Once these variables are assigned, all q_{ij} for $j \leq 4$ are set to *False* and q_{ij} for $j \geq 5$ are set to *True* by unit propagation.

In [AD08] it is shown that the width of the resolution refutation of the 3CNF encoding is unbounded. In order to use this proof we need the following definition and theorem, which combine a two-player k-pebble game with the size of the largest clause in a resolution refutation.

Definition 7.5 ([AD08]) [3] *Let F be a CNF formula. We say that the Duplicator wins the Boolean existential k-pebble game on F if there is a non-empty family H of partial truth assignments that do not falsify any clause from F such that*

(i) *If $f \in H$, then $|Dom(f)| \leq k$.*
(ii) *If $f \in H$ and $g \subseteq f$, then $g \in H$.*
(iii) *If $f \in H$, $|Dom(f)| < k$, and x is a variable, then there is some $g \in H$ such that $f \subseteq g$ and $x \in Dom(g)$.*

We say that H is a winning strategy for the Duplicator.

Theorem 7.6 ([AD08]) *Let F be a CNF formula. Then, F has a resolution refutation of width k if and only if there is no winning strategy for the Duplicator in the Boolean existential $(k + 1)$-pebble game on F.*

The proof of the non-existence of a resolution proof of fixed width for the 3CNF encoding of the pigeonhole principle in terms described above is then as follows:

Lemma 7.7 ([AD08]) *The Duplicator wins the Boolean existential $(n - 1)$-pebble game on the 3CNF encoding of the pigeonhole principle, where n is the number of pigeons.*

It follows from Lemma 7.7 that a resolution refutation of the 3CNF encoding of the pigeonhole principle will have width at least $n - 1$ for n pigeons. Without going into the details of the proof of the lemma, we observe it generalises to any encoding that contains assignment and/or regular variables only. Hence, it applies to the

---

[3]Note that this definition is closely related to the definition of k-consistency (see Definition 5.1).

interval-based regular support encoding and the order encoding of the pigeonhole principle. Since the sequential counter encoding of the at-most-one constraint is the same as the regular encoding of that problem, as shown in [ACLM10], it also cannot have a resolution proof of fixed width.

The consequence of Lemma 7.7 is that none of the encodings involving only regular and assignment variables have short resolution proofs by Corollary 3.6 in [BSW01]. Note that another consequence is that these encodings also don't have negative-hyper-resolution refutations of fixed width.

One last encoding we consider is the commander encoding (see Example 4.13). We observe that each non-assignment variable represents a statement that pigeon i is in some subset of holes. Without loss of generality, we may assume that the subsets are represented by integer intervals, i.e. a commander variable c_{ijk} will represent $p_i \geq j \wedge p_i \leq k$, where p_i represents pigeon i. Incidentally, each commander variable can be represented by a conjunction of two regular literals, say $p_{ij}^{\geq}$ and $\neg p_{i(k+1)}^{\geq}$.

Lemma 7.7 can be generalised as follows.

Lemma 7.8 ([AD08]) *Let Γ be a SAT encoding of the pigeonhole principle that contains only assignment or interval variables and encodes the standard representation of the problem[4]. Then the Duplicator wins the Boolean existential $(n-1)$-pebble game on Γ, where n is the number of pigeons.*

Proof Let B be the set of all one-to-one partial functions from $\{1, \cdots, n\}$ into $\{1, \cdots, n-1\}$. For every $a \in B$, define a partial truth assignment h_a as follows:

   (i) $h_a(p_{ij}) = 1$ if $a(i)$ is defined and $a(i) = j$,
  (ii) $h_a(p_{ij}) = 0$ if $a(i)$ is defined and $a(i) \neq j$,
 (iii) $h_a(q_{ijk}) = 0$ if $a(i)$ is defined and $a(i) \in \{j, \cdots, k\}$,
 (iv) $h_a(q_{ijk}) = 1$ if $a(i)$ is defined and $a(i) \notin \{j, \cdots, k\}$,

Let $F = \{h_a : a \in B\}$, and let H be the set of restrictions of assignments of F to all sets of at most $n - 1$ variables. It is straightforward to check that H is a winning strategy for the Duplicator: property (i) is met because, by definition, all assignments in F have at most $n - 1$ variables in the domain, property (ii) is met by definition as well, and property (iii) is met because if $h \subseteq h_a$ has at most $n - 2$ variables in its domain, then there is an empty hole. $\square$

In order to encode the pigeonhole principle one can also introduce auxiliary variables that represent a SAT formula in the original variables. Next, we present an example of such an encoding.

---

[4]This condition will become relevant later on (see Example 7.13).

Example 7.9 *Cook [Coo76] introduced the following encoding of the pigeonhole principle:*

(1) $p_{i1} \vee p_{i2} \vee \cdots \vee p_{i(n-1)}$	*for* $1 \leq i \leq n$
(2) $\neg p_{ij} \vee \neg p_{kj}$	*for* $1 \leq i \neq k \leq n$ *and* $1 \leq j \leq n-1$
(3) $p'_{ij} \leftrightarrow p_{ij} \vee (p_{i(n-1)} \wedge p_{nj})$	*for* $1 \leq i \leq n-1$ *and* $1 \leq j \leq n-2$
(4) $p''_{ij} \leftrightarrow p'_{ij} \vee (p'_{i(n-1)} \wedge p'_{nj})$	*for* $1 \leq i \leq n-2$ *and* $1 \leq j \leq n-3$

...

(n) $p_{i1}^{\prime*(n-2)} \leftrightarrow p_{i1}^{\prime*(n-3)} \vee (p_{i1}^{\prime*(n-3)} \wedge p_{21}^{\prime*(n-3)})$ *for* $1 \leq i \leq 2$

Cook's encoding allows for a resolution refutation of polynomial size. It is worth noting here that, in contrast to the SAT encodings described thus far, each new variable introduced by Cook's encoding constrains two pigeons. In particular, each non-assignment variable represents the constraint that either pigeon i is in hole j, or it is in hole $n-1$ and the nth pigeon is in hole j. Moreover, the new variables allow us to infer clauses that correspond to the inductive refutation of the pigeonhole problem. This technique, however, is hard to generalise, as it is specific to the pigeonhole problem. Examples of other extended resolution proofs can be found in [Kri85].

7.3 Experimental results

We encoded the pigeonhole principle using Cook's encoding as well as the standard, 3CNF, regular, commander and interval-based regular support encodings. We note here that the commander encoding produced the smallest number of clauses in comparison to the other encodings.

We ran all the encoded instances on the state-of-the-art clause-learning SAT-solver, MiniSAT [ES03] version 2-070721. For all of the results, the times given are elapsed times on a Lenovo 3000 N200 laptop with an Intel Core 2 Duo processor running at 1.66 GHz with 2 GB of RAM. A time limit of 20 min was set. The results are shown in Table 7.1 and Figure 7.1.

Table 7.1 MiniSAT runtimes on various encodings of the pigeonhole principle.

pigeons (n)	Cook's encoding MiniSAT (s)	standard encoding MiniSAT (s)	3CNF encoding MiniSAT (s)	regular encoding MiniSAT (s)	commander encoding MiniSAT (s)	interval-based encoding MiniSAT (s)
10	3.226	2.622	1.882	0.721	0.309	0.346
11	34.456	49.628	44.802	12.2	1.777	1.338
12	728.902	966.493	848.899	171.217	14.199	8.58
13	> 20 min	> 20 min	> 20 min	> 20 min	563.446	60.813
14	> 20 min	> 20 min	> 20 min	> 20 min	> 20 min	410.815

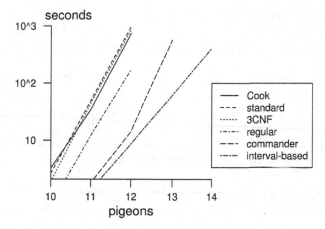

Fig. 7.1 Performance of MiniSAT on various encodings of the pigeonhole principle.

Table 7.2 MiniSAT runtimes on two variants of Cook's encoding of the pigeonhole principle.	pigeons (n)	Cook's encoding MiniSAT (s)	Cook+3CNF encoding MiniSAT (s)
	10	3.226	2.305
	11	34.456	44.356
	12	728.902	> 20 min
	13	> 20 min	> 20 min

It turns out that the interval-based regular support encoding of the pigeonhole principle is the best choice in terms of SAT-solver performance. The interesting thing about this encoding is that it has the *Helly property* [CCHS10], that is, if we take any three literals and gather clauses that contain at least two of them, such clauses will all have a literal in common.

Surprisingly enough, Cook's encoding turned out to be the worst. Even though Cook's encoding of the pigeonhole principle has a resolution proof of polynomial size, MiniSAT is not able to determine the unsatisfiability of the formula efficiently. We also ran MiniSAT on a "narrow" variant of the Cook's encoding, that is, we split the long at-least-one clauses into 3CNF by introducing auxiliary (regular) variables in the standard way. This still did not help the solver (see Table 7.2).

7.4 Theory vs. practice

Even though SAT-solvers p-simulate general resolution [PD09], there is no guarantee that such a solver will find the shortest resolution proof for a given formula in a reasonable amount of time. One reason is that there are many possible clauses that can be "learnt" by a modern SAT-solver, many of which do not belong to the shortest refutation.

Moreover, the short proof of Cook's encoding contains long clauses (of size $n-1$, $n-2$, etc.) whereas modern SAT-solvers, including MiniSAT, usually implement some method to attempt to minimise the size of learnt clauses at the conflict analysis stage.

Interestingly enough, there exists a SAT-solver called ZRes [CS00] that is able to solve pigeonhole instances with up to 20 pigeons within 20 min. It uses a ZBDD data structure [CS00] and the original Davis-Putnam (DP) [DP60] Algorithm 7.1, that is, for every variable it produces resolvents for all possible combinations of clauses that contain that variable and its negation. This method, however, is highly inefficient in general in comparison to the DPLL Algorithm 2.2.

Algorithm 7.1 The DP algorithm.

DP

    S - a set of clauses;
    while $S! = \emptyset$ or $\emptyset \notin S$ **do**
        choose_variable x;
        replace all the clauses which contain x or $\neg x$ by all resolvents on x of these clauses and
        remove all subsumed clauses;
    end while;
    if $S == \emptyset$ **then**
        return SATISFIABLE;
    end if;
    if $\emptyset \in S$ **then**
        return UNSATISFIABLE;
    end if;

7.5 Empirically good encodings

The main mechanism behind any SAT-solver is unit propagation (see Definition 2.21). Hence, as mentioned in Section 4.5, such SAT encodings are desirable that allow for a lot of information to be derived using this technique. A recent trend has been to find decompositions of global constraints into CNF that are GAC-preserving [BKNW09]. In other words, such encodings are desirable that allow the unit propagation rule to enforce the same level of consistency as a generalised-arc-consistency propagator would. It turns out that there is no GAC-preserving CNF encoding of polynomial size for the all-different constraint [BKNW09]. The proof is based on the non-existence of a monotone circuit for finding a matching in a bipartite graph. This result does not necessarily hold for the pigeonhole principle which is equivalent to finding a matching in a *complete* bipartite graph.

There are, however, SAT encodings of the pigeonhole principle on which unit propagation achieves bounds and range consistency.

Definition 7.10 ([BKN$^+$09]) *A constraint is* bound consistent *(BC) if and only if when a variable is assigned the minimum or maximum value in its domain, there* *exist compatible values between the minimum and maximum domain value for all the other variables. Such an assignment is called a* bound support.

Definition 7.11 ([BKN⁺09]) *A constraint is* range consistent *(RC) if and only if when a variable is assigned any value in its domain, there exists a bound support.*

Thus far all of the encodings were essentially translating a *particular* representation of the pigeonhole principle into SAT described below.

Example 7.12 *The pigeonhole principle can be* decomposed *into the following set of constraints* [5]:

$$p_i = 1 \vee p_i = 2 \vee \cdots \vee p_i = n - 1 \quad for\ 1 \le i \le n \qquad \text{(at-least-one constraint)}$$
$$p_i \ne p_k \qquad\qquad\qquad\qquad for\ 1 \le i < k \le n \quad \text{(at-most-one constraint)}$$

However, there exists another representation which allows for bounds- and range-consistency to be achieved on its SAT encoding. It uses the concept of the so-called *Hall intervals* (for details see [BKN⁺09]).

Example 7.13 *The pigeonhole principle can be modelled as the following 0-1 integer programming problem:*

$$p_{ilu} = 1 \qquad\qquad\qquad pigeon\ i\ is\ in\ a\ hole\ that\ belongs\ to\ the\ interval\ [l, u]$$
$$\sum_{i=1}^{n} p_{ilu} \le u - l + 1 \quad for\ 1 \le i \le n\ and\ 1 \le l \le u \le n - 1$$

It turns out that if we encode the inequalities in Example 7.13 using regular variables only, unit propagation on the resultant SAT instance will enforce bounds consistency. If we use interval variables instead, unit propagation on the resultant SAT instance will enforce range consistency [BKN⁺09].

Furthermore, by using a particular CNF encoding, a SAT-solver is actually able to solve the instances of the pigeonhole problem encoded in this way almost immediately by unit propagation.

Example 7.14 *The order encoding of the inequalities in Example 7.13 contains the following set of inconsistent clauses:*

$$p_{[11(n-1)]0}^{\le} \vee p_{[21(n-1)]0}^{\le} \vee \cdots \vee p_{[n1(n-1)]0}^{\le}$$
$$\neg p_{[i1(n-1)]0}^{\le} \ for\ 1 \le i \le n$$

where $p_{[ijk]0}^{\le}$ *denotes that the Boolean variable* $p_{[ijk]}$ *is assigned value* ≤ 0.

A SAT-solver will thus report unsatisfiability almost immediately by running unit propagation.

---

[5]Note that in the case of the regular encoding the at-most-one constraint is $h_i \ne h_k$ (see Example 7.3), where each h_i represents a hole and $1 \le i < k \le n - 1$.

This example shows the influence of the problem specification *before* it's encoded into SAT. It also shows the importance of choosing the right *decomposition* of global constraints. In the case of the pigeonhole problem it is the choice of a decomposition of the all-different constraint that influences SAT-solver performance the most. If we decompose it into at-least-one and at-most-one constraints, their SAT encodings will be very inefficient. If we use the decomposition presented in Example 7.13 instead, SAT-solvers are likely to solve encodings of this representation much more quickly.

7.6 Summary

In this chapter we compared various SAT encodings of CSP instances on the example of the pigeonhole principle. We have shown that the new variables introduced in the sequential counter, 3CNF, regular and order encodings are in fact regular ones. We have also shown that the commander variables can be represented in terms of regular ones.

We have also provided a theoretical reason why none of the general SAT encodings will produce short extended resolution proofs for the pigeonhole principle. Hence, modern clause-learning SAT-solvers might not solve them efficiently for this reason. This is in contrast to constraint solvers which provide propagators for the global all-different constraint by which the pigeonhole principle can be modelled. The Minion solver, for instance, performs a check on whether the number of available domain values is greater than or equal to the number of variables constrained by the all-different constraint. Hence, it is able to detect the unsatisfiability of the pigeonhole principle almost immediately. It is worth mentioning that a similar technique has been used in a SAT-based constraint solver called Sugar [TTKB09] which uses the order encoding.

Since SAT-solvers *p*-simulate general resolution [PD09], those encodings are desirable that translate a CSP instance into a SAT formula that has a short resolution proof (see Section 4.5). In the case of the pigeonhole principle, such an encoding turned out not to be the best choice, as shown in Section 7.4. However, the idea of introducing auxiliary variables to possibly reduce the resolution proof size has gained some attention in the last few years [SB06, AKS10].

So far there has been little success in integrating the extended resolution rule in a SAT-solver. The problem lies in finding appropriate auxiliary variables that would aid the solver in finding a satisfiable assignment. Due to the diversity of constraints available there is no general rule which specifies what sort of new variables will help prune the search space. Nevertheless, a few attempts have been made [AKS10].

In this chapter we have also shown the importance of choosing the right problem specification *before* encoding it into SAT. In particular, we showed the influence of choosing the right *decomposition* of all-different for the pigeonhole problem.

Chapter 8
Conclusions

"Poirot," I said. "I have been thinking."
"An admirable exercise my friend. Continue it."

Agatha Christie

8.1 Summary of contributions

It is well-known that SAT-solvers are remarkably efficient. However, little is known as to why this is the case. In this book we have tried to answer this question by investigating the connections between *constraint satisfaction* and *Boolean satisfiability* problems.

Various techniques have been developed to solve instances of CSP and SAT. Usually these interleave *constraint propagation* with *search*. Constraint solvers often implement several propagation techniques, which are targeted at solving specific constraints (see Section 2.2.2). In the case of modern SAT-solvers, unit propagation and the so-called *conflict-driven clause learning with restarts* play the key roles in the solving process (see Section 2.4).

Since SAT can actually be viewed as a subset of CSP, there are many similarities in the study of these two types of problems. With regards to solver performance, the impact of variable and value orderings has been investigated (see Section 2.2.1). Non-chronological backtracking as well as some forms of learning have been applied in solving instances of both CSP and SAT. However, the influence of such techniques on solver performance in SAT and CSP solving has been significantly different. In particular, conflict-driven clause learning (see Section 2.4.3) has led to remarkable time improvements in SAT-solving, whereas a similar nogood learning technique in CSP has led to minor improvements if any. Moreover, value orderings don't have as much impact in SAT solving as they do in CSP solving simply because Boolean variables can take only two values in contrast to constraint problems where the domains can be arbitrarily large.

Although there exist many similarities between CSP and SAT, the translation of ideas between constraint satisfaction and Boolean satisfiability is not as straightforward as one might think. First, the two communities differ in their basic approaches to problem solving. Constraint solvers aim to allow the user to tune the solver

© Springer International Publishing Switzerland 2015
J. Petke, *Bridging Constraint Satisfaction and Boolean Satisfiability*,
Artificial Intelligence: Foundations, Theory, and Algorithms,
DOI 10.1007/978-3-319-21810-6_8

for specific problem purposes, whereas SAT-solvers generally act as a black box. Secondly, input to a constraint solver is usually very similar to the real-world description of the problem. If, for instance, we want to impose the not-all-equal constraint on a set of three variables, we could simply write not-all-equal(v_1, v_2, v_3). SAT-solver input is very restrictive, since there is one specific model one can use, that is CNF. On the other hand, there is no such standard input language for constraint solvers which sometimes makes CSP-solver comparison and the use of such solvers not as appealing as in the case of SAT. Furthermore, there have been few changes in the core algorithm of SAT-solvers since the invention of the DPLL algorithm in the 1960s. The development of constraint solvers, on the other hand, has been much more dynamic and varied (see Section 2.2).

Moreover, in the theoretical literature there are some ideas for boosting solver performance that have not yet been implemented. One example is the identification of tractability in a CSP problem. *Tractable* CSP instances are those instances for which an algorithm exists that decides their satisfiability in polynomial-time. There exists such an algorithm, for example, for CSP instances whose structure has bounded-width [CCJ94]. Information about the structure of CSP instance has started to be explored in the Toolbar2 MaxCSP solver [SBdG⁺08]. However, finding such tractable structures might not be the best idea in some cases due to time and space requirements. Thus the performance gain might not be worth it. Another reason why some theoretical findings have not been implemented in practice is the constraint solver architecture. The constraints "talk to each other" through variable domains. Hence, there is no way of using some possible information about overlapping constraints in current constraint solvers.

The results presented in Chapter 3 have established that *in order to improve the performance of constraint solvers we could use benchmarks which can explore that performance over a range of different problem types with different characteristics*. One way to systematically develop such benchmarks is to use the insights from the theoretical study of constraint satisfaction. Benchmarks derived in this way can be simple enough to analyse in detail, and yet challenging enough to reveal specific weaknesses in solver techniques.

There are, however, a few problems in producing useful benchmarks for constraint solvers. One such difficulty is the fact that there is no standard input format for CSP-solvers. Thus it often happens that running a constraint solver on two different models of the given problem leads to significantly different runtimes. Another issue that needs to be considered is the translation effort from the user-specified input in a high-level language to a lower-level language that is essentially used by the solver. One such translator is Tailor which provides the transition between the Essence' and Minion input formats. During the translation process certain features of the given problem might get lost. Hence we suggest that a better awareness of the factors of a problem specification that can ensure tractability could lead to better translation software, which ensures that such features are preserved. For instance, identification of tractable parts of a problem instance at the pre-processing stage could help a constraint solver to exploit those during the solving process.

It is worth mentioning that in the case of SAT-solvers solver comparison is relatively easy due to the standardised input language. However, also here the question of loss of information arises at the translation stage into CNF. When translating into SAT a tractable instance might suddenly become very hard to solve, or its "nice" structure might be completely lost. Moreover, SAT encodings often produce a huge set of clauses. Thus space requirements are frequently an issue when using SAT-solvers to decide the satisfiability of problems defined on large domains.

Even though translating into SAT may be expensive in terms of time and space, experimental results in Chapter 3 have revealed that *SAT-based constraint solvers are sometimes much more efficient than conventional solvers on certain families of CSP instances* (see Section 3.2 and 3.6). Interestingly enough, such SAT-based solvers did quite well in CSP-solver competitions. They even performed well on the problem instances containing highly structured so-called global constraints, which are said to be the natural domain of CSP-solvers.

In order to explain the remarkable efficiency of SAT-solvers on certain classes of CSP instances, we have first presented the different ways in which a CSP instance can be translated into SAT in Chapter 4. We note that comparison of various SAT encodings is difficult, since it is hard to identify features of a SAT encoding that are "good" in all cases. Most comparisons thus far have been purely empirical. In Chapter 4 we have presented a few desirable features which unfortunately do not always lead to improvements in SAT-solver performance. From the point of view of the practitioner a "good" SAT encoding would allow the solver to make as many deductions as possible and be as compact as possible. Another desirable feature is high solution density of satisfiable instances. Since SAT-solvers p-simulate general resolution, SAT encodings with short resolution proofs are also desirable. There is, however, no one property that would allow us to decide if one encoding is better than another for all possible problem instances. Nevertheless, we have managed to identify which encodings are "good" for some particular classes of CSP instances.

In Chapter 5 we have shown the *satisfiability of the direct encoding of a certain class of CSP instances will be decided by a clause-learning randomised SAT-solver in expected polynomial-time*. We considered those instances whose unsatisfiability can be proved by enforcing a fixed level of consistency. This result has been proved by combining two concepts, one from the area of constraint satisfaction and the other from the area of Boolean satisfiability. In particular, we have connected k-consistency to a certain SAT inference rule called negative-hyper-resolution. Furthermore, we have established a connection between SAT-solver performance and the existence of a negative-hyper-resolution refutation of fixed width. By combining these two results we have shown that a clause-learning SAT-solver with a purely random branching strategy will simulate the effect of enforcing k-consistency in expected polynomial-time, for all fixed k (see Theorem 5.20). This is sufficient to ensure that such solvers are able to solve certain problem families much more efficiently than conventional CSP-solvers relying on domain propagation. We have also performed an experimental evaluation of our results. These have shown that *clause-learning SAT-solvers are even more efficient than our theoretical results suggest* (see Section 5.5).

In Chapter 6 we have made another contribution towards answering the question about the efficiency of modern SAT-solvers. It has to do with the right choice of an encoding for certain tractable families of CSP instances. In particular, *we have given a theoretical argument for the choice of the order encoding (see Section 6.3) over other standard ones* which has been validated in our experiments in Section 6.5. We considered the following tractable classes of CSP instances: constant-closed (see Section 3.2), max-closed (see Section 3.3) and connected-row-convex (see Section 3.5). It turns out that translating such instances using the order encoding results in SAT formulae that fall into known tractable language classes of SAT, whereas this is not true for either sparse encodings or the log encoding. Moreover, *we have given a complete list of all constraint types which are encoded to tractable language classes for SAT using the order encoding.*

Taking into account our results from the previous chapters, we have compared several SAT encodings of the famous problem of the pigeonhole principle in Chapter 7. We have provided a theoretical and empirical evaluation. In particular, *we have provided a theoretical argument why none of the encodings considered (except for Cook's encoding) are likely to allow a SAT-solver to decide the unsatisfiability of the pigeonhole principle efficiently.* We have shown that such encodings produce resolution refutations of exponential size. It turns out that even though Cook's encoding of the problem has a short resolution proof, SAT-solvers do not perform well on such an encoding. One reason might be that modern SAT-solvers prioritize short clauses at the clause-learning stage and Cook's proof requires long clauses. Another issue is that even though SAT-solvers p-simulate general resolution, a particular proof can be difficult to find due to the random behaviour implemented in modern solvers. This example clearly shows the gap between theoretical results and practical applications. Moreover, *we have shown that the auxiliary variables introduced in the various encodings represent essentially the same domain restrictions.*

On the example of the pigeonhole principle we have shown that even though SAT-solvers are indeed extremely efficient there exist CSP instances for which using constraint solvers is sometimes a far better choice.

8.2   Open questions

- Which concepts from the area of CSP can be transferred into SAT and vice versa?

  - How can the 2-watched-literals scheme, used in SAT-solvers (see Section 2.4.2), be generalised into solving arbitrary constraints?
  - How to efficiently incorporate a form of nogood learning into constraint solvers? What would be a useful nogood for a particular constraint, like the inequality constraint?

- Which encodings should be chosen for translating CSP instances into SAT?

  – What are the "good" features of SAT encodings of instances belonging to certain CSP classes? Is one of these "good" features the Helly property (see Section 7.3)?
  – Which SAT encodings are best for particular classes of CSP instances, like the class of submodular constraints [ŽJ10]?
  – How can extended resolution be exploited in SAT-solvers? What sort of auxiliary variables would be useful to introduce during the solving process?

- When is it better to use a SAT-solver instead of a CSP-solver and vice versa?

  – What features of instances can current clause-learning SAT-solvers exploit (aside from bounded-width structures)?
  – What features of instances are exploited by conventional constraint solvers?
  – When is it better to use a hybrid solver or an SMT-solver instead of a SAT or CSP-solver? Can we answer this question empirically by using real-world benchmarks, for instance, from the area of software verification?

- How to solve tractable sub-parts of CSP problems efficiently?

  – What's the best way of identifying tractable sub-parts of CSP problems, like the max-closed constraints?
  – How to utilize the identification of tractable subproblems in SAT-solvers? Would it be useful to identify tractable structures in the graph of an input instance at the pre-processing stage?

- What is the best way of translating a CSP instance into the input format for a particular solver?

  – Could a standardised input format for CSP problems help improve constraint solver performance?

Bibliography

[ABD07]   A. Atserias, A.A. Bulatov, and V. Dalmau. On the power of k-consistency. In *Proceedings of the 34th International Colloquium on Automata, Languages and Programming - ICALP 2007*, volume 4596 of *Lecture Notes in Computer Science*, pages 279–290. Springer, 2007.

[ACLM08a]   J. Argelich, A. Cabiscol, I. Lynce, and F. Manyà. Encoding Max-CSP into partial Max-SAT. In *Proceedings of the 38th IEEE International Symposium on Multiple-Valued Logic - ISMVL 2008*, pages 106–111. IEEE Computer Society, 2008.

[ACLM08b]   J. Argelich, A. Cabiscol, I. Lynce, and F. Manyà. Modelling Max-CSP as partial Max-SAT. In *Proceedings of the 11th International Conference on Theory and Applications of Satisfiability Testing - SAT 2008*, volume 4996 of *Lecture Notes in Computer Science*, pages 1–14. Springer, 2008.

[ACLM09]   J. Argelich, A. Cabiscol, I. Lynce, and F. Manyà. Regular encodings from Max-CSP into partial Max-SAT. In *Proceedings of the 39th International Symposium on Multiple-Valued Logic - ISMVL 2009*, pages 196–202. IEEE Computer Society, 2009.

[ACLM10]   J. Argelich, A. Cabiscol, I. Lynce, and F. Manyà. New insights into encodings from MaxCSP into partial MaxSAT. In *Proceedings of the 40th IEEE International Symposium on Multiple-Valued Logic - ISMVL 2010*, pages 46–52. IEEE Computer Society, 2010.

[ACLM12]   J. Argelich, A. Cabiscol, I. Lynce, and F. Manyà. Efficient encodings from CSP into SAT, and from MaxCSP into MaxSAT. *Multiple-Valued Logic and Soft Computing*, 19(1-3):3–23, 2012.

[AD08]   A. Atserias and V. Dalmau. A combinatorial characterization of resolution width. *Journal of Computer and System Sciences*, 74(3):323–334, 2008.

[AFT11]   A. Atserias, J.K. Fichte, and M. Thurley. Clause-learning algorithms with many restarts and bounded-width resolution. *Journal of Artificial Intelligence Research*, 40:353–373, 2011.

[AKS10]   G. Audemard, G. Katsirelos, and L. Simon. A restriction of extended resolution for clause learning SAT solvers. In *Proceedings of the 24th AAAI Conference on Artificial Intelligence - AAAI 2010*, pages 15–20. AAAI Press, 2010.

[AM04]   C. Ansótegui and F. Manyà. Mapping problems with finite-domain variables into problems with Boolean variables. In *Proceedings of the 17th International Conference on Theory and Applications of Satisfiability Testing - SAT 2004*, volume 3542 of *Lecture Notes in Computer Science*, pages 1–15. Springer, 2004.

© Springer International Publishing Switzerland 2015   105
J. Petke, *Bridging Constraint Satisfaction and Boolean Satisfiability*,
Artificial Intelligence: Foundations, Theory, and Algorithms,
DOI 10.1007/978-3-319-21810-6

[AMS03]   F.A. Aloul, I.L. Markov, and K.A. Sakallah.   Shatter: Efficient symmetry-
            breaking for Boolean satisfiability. In *Proceedings of the 40th Design Automation
            Conference - DAC 2003*, pages 836–839. ACM, 2003.

[Bac07]   F. Bacchus. GAC via unit propagation. In *Proceedings of the 13th International
            Conference on Principles and Practice of Constraint Programming - CP 2007*,
            volume 4741 of *Lecture Notes in Computer Science*, pages 133–147. Springer,
            2007.

[Bak95]   A.B. Baker. *Intelligent Backtracking on Constraint Satisfaction Problems: Exper-
            imental and Theoretical Results*. PhD thesis, University of Oregon, 1995.

[BBR09]   O. Bailleux, Y. Boufkhad, and O. Roussel. New encodings of pseudo-Boolean
            constraints into CNF. In *Proccedings of the 12th International Conference on
            Theory and Applications of Satisfiability Testing - SAT 2009*, volume 5584 of
            Lecture Notes in Computer Science, pages 181–194. Springer, 2009.

[Bes06]   C. Bessière. Constraint propagation. In F. Rossi, P. van Beek, and T. Walsh, editors,
            Handbook of Constraint Programming, chapter 3, pages 29–83. Elsevier, 2006.

[BHLS04]   F. Boussemart, F. Hemery, C. Lecoutre, and L. Sais. Boosting systematic search
            by weighting constraints. In *Proceedings of the 16th European Conference on
            Artificial Intelligence - ECAI 2004*, pages 146–150. IOS Press, 2004.

[BHZ06]   L. Bordeaux, Y. Hamadi, and L. Zhang. Propositional satisfiability and constraint
            programming: A comparative survey. *ACM Computing Surveys*, 38(4):1–62, 2006.

[BK09]   L. Barto and M. Kozik. Constraint satisfaction problems of bounded width. In
            *Proceedings of the 50th Annual IEEE Symposium on Foundations of Computer
            Science - FOCS 2009*, pages 595–603. IEEE Computer Society, 2009.

[BKJ05]   A. Bulatov, A. Krokhin, and P. Jeavons. Classifying the complexity of constraints
            using finite algebras. *SIAM Journal on Computing*, 34(3):720–742, 2005.

[BKN+09]   C. Bessière, G. Katsirelos, N. Narodytska, C.-G. Quimper, and T. Walsh. Decom-
            positions of all different, global cardinality and related constraints. In *Proceedings
            of the 21st International Joint Conference on Artificial Intelligence - IJCAI 2009*,
            pages 419–424. AAAI Press, 2009.

[BKNW09]   C. Bessière, G. Katsirelos, N. Narodytska, and T. Walsh. Circuit complexity and
            decompositions of global constraints. In *Proceedings of the 21st International
            Joint Conference on Artificial Intelligence - IJCAI 2009*, pages 412–418. AAAI
            Press, 2009.

[BKS04]   P. Beame, H.A. Kautz, and A. Sabharwal. Towards understanding and harnessing
            the potential of clause learning. *Journal of Artificial Intelligence Research*,
            22:319–351, 2004.

[BL99]   H.K. Büning and T. Lettmann. *Propositional logic: deduction and algorithms*.
            Cambridge Tracts in Theoretical Computer Science. Cambridge University Press,
            1999.

[Bod08]   M. Bodirsky.   Constraint satisfaction problems with infinite templates.   In
            Complexity of Constraints, volume 5250 of *Lecture Notes in Computer Science*,
            pages 196–228. Springer, 2008.

[BR97]   C. Bessière and J.-C. Régin. Arc consistency for general constraint networks:
            preliminary results. In *Proceedings of the 15th International Joint Conference
            on Artificial Intelligence - IJCAI 1997*, pages 398–404. Morgan Kaufmann, 1997.

[BRYZ05]   C. Bessière, J.-C. Régin, R.H.C. Yap, and Y. Zhang. An optimal coarse-grained
            arc consistency algorithm. *Artificial Intelligence*, 165(2):165–185, 2005.

[BS97]   R.J. Bayardo and R.C. Schrag. Using CSP look-back techniques to solve real-
            world SAT instances. In *Proceedings of the 14th National (US) Conference on
            Artificial Intelligence - AAAI 1997, and 9th Innovative Applications of Artificial
            Intelligence Conference - IAAI 1997*, pages 203–208. AAAI Press / The MIT Press,
            1997.

[BSW01]   E. Ben-Sasson and A. Wigderson. Short proofs are narrow - resolution made
            simple. *Journal of the ACM*, 48(2):149–169, 2001.

[Bul06]   A.A. Bulatov. A dichotomy theorem for constraint satisfaction problems on a 3-element set. *Journal of the ACM*, 53(1):66–120, 2006.

[BV08]   A.A. Bulatov and M. Valeriote. Recent results on the algebraic approach to the CSP. In *Complexity of Constraints*, volume 5250 of *Lecture Notes in Computer Science*, pages 68–92. Springer, 2008.

[CBA05]   M. Correia, P. Barahona, and F. Azevedo. CaSPER: A programming environment for development and integration of constraint solvers. In *Proceedings of the 1st International Workshop on Constraint Programming Beyond Finite Integer Domains - BeyondFD 2005*, pages 59–73. Software available at http://proteina.di.fct.unl.pt/casper, 2005.

[CCHS10]   V. Chepoi, N. Creignou, M. Hermann, and G. Salzer. The Helly property and satisfiability of Boolean formulas defined on set families. *European Journal of Combinatorics*, 31(2):502–516, 2010.

[CCJ94]   M.C. Cooper, D.A. Cohen, and P. Jeavons. Characterising tractable constraints. *Artificial Intelligence*, 65:347–361, 1994.

[CDG11]   H. Chen, V. Dalmau, and B. Grußien. Arc consistency and friends. *Computing Research Repository - CoRR*, abs/1104.4993, 2011.

[CFG⁺96]   D.A. Clark, J. Frank, I.P. Gent, E. MacIntyre, N. Tomov, and T. Walsh. Local search and the number of solutions. In *Proceedings of the 2nd International Conference on Principles and Practice of Constraint Programming, - CP 1996*, volume 1118 of *Lecture Notes in Computer Science*, pages 119–133. Springer, 1996.

[CHOCot08] The CHOCO team. Choco: an open source Java constraint programming library. In *Proceedings of the 3rd International CSP Solver Competition*, pages 7–14, 2008. Software available at http://www.emn.fr/z-info/choco-solver/.

[CJ06]   D.A. Cohen and P. Jeavons. The complexity of constraint languages. In F. Rossi, P. van Beek, and T. Walsh, editors, *Handbook of Constraint Programming*, chapter 8, pages 245–280. Elsevier, 2006.

[CJG08]   D.A. Cohen, P. Jeavons, and M. Gyssens. A unified theory of structural tractability for constraint satisfaction problems. *Journal of Computer and System Sciences*, 74(5):721–743, 2008.

[CJJ⁺06]   D.A. Cohen, P. Jeavons, C. Jefferson, K.E. Petrie, and B.M. Smith. Symmetry definitions for constraint satisfaction problems. *Constraints*, 11(2–3):115–137, 2006.

[CJJK00]   D.A. Cohen, P. Jeavons, P. Jonsson, and M. Koubarakis. Building tractable disjunctive constraints. *Journal of the ACM*, 47(5):826–853, 2000.

[CKS01]   N. Creignou, S. Khanna, and M. Sudan. *Complexity Classification of Boolean Constraint Satisfaction Problems*, volume 7 of *SIAM Monographs on Discrete Mathematics and Applications*. Society for Industrial and Applied Mathematics, 2001.

[Coh04]   D.A. Cohen. Tractable decision for a constraint language implies tractable search. *Constraints*, 9(3):219–229, 2004.

[Coo71]   S.A. Cook. The complexity of theorem-proving procedures. In *Proceedings of the 3rd Annual ACM Symposium on Theory of Computing - STOC 1971*, pages 151–158. ACM, 1971.

[Coo76]   S.A. Cook. A short proof of the pigeon hole principle using extended resolution. *SIGACT News*, 8(4):28–32, 1976.

[Coo89]   M.C. Cooper. An optimal k-consistency algorithm. *Artificial Intelligence*, 41(1):89–95, 1989.

[CR97]   C. Chekuri and A. Rajaraman. Conjunctive query containment revisited. In *Proceedings of the 6th International Conference on Database Theory - ICDT 1997*, pages 56–70, 1997.

[CS00]   P. Chatalic and L. Simon. ZRES: The old Davis-Putman procedure meets ZBDD. In *Proceedings of the 17th International Conference on Automated Deduction - CADE 2000*, volume 1831 of *Lecture Notes in Computer Science*, pages 449–454. Springer, 2000.

[CvB01]   X. Chen and P. van Beek. Conflict-directed backjumping revisited. *Journal of Artificial Intelligence Research*, 14:53–81, 2001.

[DB97]   R. Debruyne and C. Bessière. Some practicable filtering techniques for the constraint satisfaction problem. In *Proceedings of the 15th International Joint Conference on Artificial Intelligence - IJCAI 1997*, pages 412–417. Morgan Kaufmann, 1997.

[DB05]   R. Debruyne and C. Bessière. Optimal and suboptimal singleton arc consistency algorithms. In *Proceedings of the 19th International Joint Conference on Artificial Intelligence - IJCAI 2005*, pages 54–59. Professional Book Center, 2005.

[DBvH99]   Y. Deville, O. Barette, and P. van Hentenryck. Constraint satisfaction over connected row convex constraints. *Artificial Intelligence*, 109(1–2):243–271, 1999.

[Dec92]   R. Dechter. From local to global consistency. *Artificial Intelligence*, 55(1):87–107, 1992.

[Dec06]   R. Dechter. Tractable structures for CSPs. In F. Rossi, P. van Beek, and T. Walsh, editors, *Handbook of Constraint Programming*, chapter 7, pages 209–244. Elsevier, 2006.

[DF02]   R. Dechter and D. Frost. Backjump-based backtracking for constraint satisfaction problems. *Artificial Intelligence*, 136(2):147–188, 2002.

[DG84]   W.F. Dowling and J.H. Gallier. Linear-time algorithms for testing the satisfiability of propositional Horn formulae. *Journal of Logic Programming*, 1(3):267–284, 1984.

[dK89]   J. de Kleer. A comparison of ATMS and CSP techniques. In *Proceedings of the 11th International Joint Conference on Artificial Intelligence - IJCAI 1989*, pages 290–296. Morgan Kaufmann, 1989.

[DKV02]   V. Dalmau, P.G. Kolaitis, and M.Y. Vardi. Constraint satisfaction, bounded treewidth, and finite-variable logics. In *Proceedings of the 8th International Conference on Constraint Programming - CP 2002*, volume 2470 of *Lecture Notes in Computer Science*, pages 310–326. Springer, 2002.

[DLL62]   M. Davis, G. Logemann, and D.W. Loveland. A machine program for theorem-proving. *Commun. ACM*, 5(7):394–397, 1962.

[DP60]   M. Davis and H. Putnam. A computing procedure for quantification theory. *Journal of the ACM*, 7(3):201–215, 1960.

[DP87]   R. Dechter and J. Pearl. Network-based heuristics for constraint satisfaction problems. *Artificial Intelligence*, 34(1):1–38, 1987.

[DP89]   R. Dechter and J. Pearl. Tree clustering for constraint networks. *Artificial Intelligence*, 38(3):353–366, 1989.

[ES03]   N. Eén and N. Sörensson. An extensible SAT-solver. In *Proceedings of the 6th International Conference on Theory and Applications of Satisfiability Testing - SAT 2003*, volume 2919 of *Lecture Notes in Computer Science*, pages 502–518. Springer, 2003.

[FD95]   D. Frost and R. Dechter. Look-ahead value ordering for constraint satisfaction problems. In *Proceedings of the 14th International Joint Conference on Artificial Intelligence - IJCAI 1995*, pages 572–578. Morgan Kaufmann, 1995.

[FG10]   A.M. Frisch and P.A. Giannoro. SAT encodings of the at-most-k constraint. In *Proceedings of the 9th International Workshop on Constraint Modelling and Reformulation - ModRef 2010*, 2010.

[FGJ+07]   A.M. Frisch, M. Grum, C. Jefferson, B. Martínez Hernández, and I. Miguel. The design of ESSENCE: A constraint language for specifying combinatorial problems. In *Proceedings of the 20th International Joint Conference on Artificial Intelligence - IJCAI 2007*, pages 80–87. AAAI Press, 2007.

[FM06]   E.C. Freuder and A.K. Mackworth. Constraint satisfaction: An emerging paradigm. In F. Rossi, P. van Beek, and T. Walsh, editors, *Handbook of Constraint Programming*, chapter 2, pages 13–28. Elsevier, 2006.

[FM09]   J. Franco and J. Martin. A history of satisfiability. In A. Biere, M.J.H. Heule, H. van Maaren, and T. Walsh, editors, *Handbook of Satisfiability*, volume 185 of *Frontiers in Artificial Intelligence and Applications*, pages 3–74. IOS Press, 2009.

[Fre78]   E.C. Freuder. Synthesizing constraint expressions. *Communications of the ACM*, 21(11):958–966, 1978.

[Fre82]   E.C. Freuder. A sufficient condition for backtrack-free search. *Journal of the ACM*, 29(1):24–32, 1982.

[Fre85]   E.C. Freuder. A sufficient condition for backtrack-bounded search. *Journal of the ACM*, 32(4):755–761, 1985.

[Fre90]   E.C. Freuder. Complexity of k-tree structured constraint satisfaction problems. In *Proceedings of the 8th National (US) Conference on Artificial Intelligence*, pages 4–9. AAAI Press, 1990.

[FS09]   T. Feydy and P.J. Stuckey. Lazy clause generation reengineered. In *Proceedings of the 15th International Conference on Principles and Practice of Constraint Programming*, volume 5732 of *Lecture Notes in Computer Science*, pages 352–366. Springer, 2009.

[FV98]   T. Feder and M.Y. Vardi. The computational structure of monotone monadic SNP and constraint satisfaction: A study through Datalog and group theory. *SIAM Journal on Computing*, 28(1):57–104, 1998.

[FW92]   E.C. Freuder and R. Wallace. Partial constraint satisfaction. *Artificial Intelligence*, 58(1–3):21–70, 1992.

[GB65]   S.W. Golomb and L.D. Baumert. Backtrack programming. *Journal of the ACM*, 12(4):516–524, 1965.

[Gen02]   I.P. Gent. Arc consistency in SAT. In *Proceedings of the 15th European Conference on Artificial Intelligence - ECAI 2002*, pages 121–125. IOS Press, 2002.

[GJ08]   M.J. Green and C. Jefferson. Structural tractability of propagated constraints. In *Proceedings of the 14th International Conference on Constraint Programming - CP 2008*, volume 5202 of *Lecture Notes in Computer Science*, pages 372–386. Springer, 2008.

[GJC94]   M. Gyssens, P. Jeavons, and D.A. Cohen. Decomposing constraint satisfaction problems using database techniques. *Artificial Intelligence*, 66(1):57–89, 1994.

[GJM06]   I.P. Gent, C. Jefferson, and I. Miguel. Minion: A fast scalable constraint solver. In *Proceedings of the 17th European Conference on Artificial Intelligence - ECAI 2006*, pages 98–102. IOS Press, 2006. Software available at http://minion. sourceforge.net/.

[GJMN07]   I.P. Gent, C. Jefferson, I. Miguel, and P. Nightingale. Data structures for generalised arc consistency for extensional constraints. In *Proceedings of the 22nd AAAI Conference on Artificial Intelligence*, pages 191–197. AAAI Press, 2007.

[GLS00]   G. Gottlob, N. Leone, and F. Scarcello. A comparison of structural CSP decomposition methods. *Artificial Intelligence*, 124(2):243–282, 2000.

[GMR08]   I.P. Gent, I. Miguel, and A. Rendl. Common subexpression elimination in automated constraint modelling. In *Proceedings of the 2008 Workshop on Modelling and Solving Problems with Constraints*, pages 24–30, 2008. Software available at http://www.cs.st-andrews.ac.uk/$\sim$andrea/tailor/.

[GN02]   E. Goldberg and Y. Novikov. BerkMin: A fast and robust SAT-solver. In *Proceedings of the 2002 Design, Automation and Test in Europe Conference and Exposition - DATE 2002*, pages 142–149. IEEE Computer Society, 2002.

[GN04]   I.P. Gent and P. Nightingale. A new encoding of AllDifferent into SAT. In *Proceedings of the 3rd International Workshop on Modelling and Reformulating Constraint Satisfaction Problems - ModRef 2004*, 2004.

[GPFW96]   J. Gu, P. W. Purdom, J. Franco, and B. W. Wah. Algorithms for the satisfiability problem: A survey. In *DIMACS*, Series in Discrete Mathematics and Theoretical Computer Science, pages 19–152. American Mathematical Society, 1996.

[Gro06]   M. Grohe.   The structure of tractable constraint satisfaction problems.   In
            *Proceedings of the 31st International Symposium on Mathematical Foundations
            of Computer Science - MFCS 2006*, volume 4162 of *Lecture Notes in Computer
            Science*, pages 58–72. Springer, 2006.
[Gro07]   M. Grohe. The complexity of homomorphism and constraint satisfaction problems
            seen from the other side. *Journal of the ACM*, 54(1):1–24, 2007.
[GSK98]   C. P. Gomes, B. Selman, and H.A. Kautz.   Boosting combinatorial search
            through randomization.   In *Proceedings of the 15th National Conference on
            Artificial Intelligence - AAAI 1998, and 10th Innovative Applications of Artificial
            Intelligence Conference - IAAI 1998*, pages 431–437. AAAI Press / The MIT Press,
            1998.
[HE80]   R.M. Haralick and G.L. Elliott. Increasing tree search efficiency for constraint
            satisfaction problems. *Artificial Intelligence*, 14(3):263–313, 1980.
[HL88]   C.-C. Han and C.-H. Lee. Comments on Mohr and Henderson's path consistency
            algorithm. *Artificial Intelligence*, 36(1):125–130, 1988.
[HM05]   J. Hwang and D.G. Mitchell. 2-way vs. d-way branching for CSP. In *Proceedings
            of the 11th International Conference on Principles and Practice of Constraint
            Programming - CP 2005*, volume 3709 of *Lecture Notes in Computer Science*,
            pages 343–357. Springer, 2005.
[Hoo99]   H.H. Hoos. SAT-encodings, search space structure, and local search performance.
            In *Proceedings of the 16th International Joint Conference on Artificial Intelligence
            - IJCAI 1999*, pages 296–303. Morgan Kaufmann, 1999.
[Hoo07]   J.N. Hooker.   *Integrated Methods for Optimization*.   International Series in
            Operations Research & Management Science. Springer, 2007.
[HT06]   H.H. Hoos and E. Tsang. Local search methods. In F. Rossi, P. van Beek, and
            T. Walsh, editors, *Handbook of Constraint Programming*, chapter 5, pages 135–
            167. Elsevier, 2006.
[Hua08]   J. Huang.   Universal Booleanization of constraint models.   In *Proceedings
            of the 14th International Conference on Principles and Practice of Constraint
            Programming - CP 2008*, volume 5202 of *Lecture Notes in Computer Science*,
            pages 144–158. Springer, 2008. Software available at http://users.rsise.anu.edu.au/
            $\sim$jinbo/fzntini/.
[JC95]   P. Jeavons and M.C. Cooper. Tractable constraints on ordered domains. *Artificial
            Intelligence*, 79(2):327–339, 1995.
[JCG97]   P. Jeavons, D.A. Cohen, and M. Gyssens. Closure properties of constraints. *Journal
            of the ACM*, 44(4):527–548, 1997.
[JT03]   P. Jégou and C. Terrioux. Hybrid backtracking bounded by tree-decomposition of
            constraint networks. *Artificial Intelligence*, 146(1):43–75, 2003.
[Kri85]   B. Krishnamurthy. Short proofs for tricky formulas. *Acta Informatica*, 22(3):253–
            275, 1985.
[Kum92]   V. Kumar. Algorithms for constraint satisfaction problems: A survey. *AI Magazine*,
            13(1):32–44, 1992.
[KV00a]   P.G. Kolaitis and M.Y. Vardi.   Conjunctive-query containment and constraint
            satisfaction. *Journal of Computer and System Sciences*, 61:302–332, 2000.
[KV00b]   P.G. Kolaitis and M.Y. Vardi. A game-theoretic approach to constraint satisfaction.
            In *Proceedings of the 17th National (US) Conference on Artificial Intellignece
            - AAAI 2000, and 12th Conference on Innovative Applications of Artificial
            Intelligence - IAAI 2000*, pages 175–181. AAAI Press / The MIT Press, 2000.
[LBH04]   C. Lecoutre, F. Boussemart, and F. Hemery.   Backjump-based techniques versus
            conflict-directed heuristics.   In *Proceedings of the 16th IEEE International
            Conference on Tools with Artificial Intelligence - ICTAI 2004*, pages 549–557.
            IEEE Computer Society, 2004.
[LMS01]   I. Lynce and J. Marques-Silva. The puzzling role of simplification in propositional
            satisfiability. In *Proceedings of the 2001 EPIA Workshop on Constraint Satis-*

faction and Operational Research Techniques for Problem Solving - EPIA-CSOR 2001, pages 73–86, 2001.

[LSTV07]   C. Lecoutre, L. Sais, S. Tabary, and V. Vidal. Recording and minimizing nogoods from restarts. *Journal on Satisfiability, Boolean Modeling and Computation*, 1(3–4):147–167, 2007.

[LT06]   C. Lecoutre and S. Tabary. Abscon 109 A generic CSP solver. In *Proceedings of the 2nd International CSP Solver Competition*, pages 55–63, 2006. Software available at http://www.cril.univ-artois.fr/~lecoutre/software.html.

[Mac77]   A.K. Mackworth. Consistency in networks of relations. *Artificial Intelligence*, 8(1):99–118, 1977.

[MH86]   R. Mohr and T.C. Henderson. Arc and path consistency revisited. *Artificial Intelligence*, 28(2):225–233, 1986.

[MMZ$^+$01] M.W. Moskewicz, C.F. Madigan, Y. Zhao, L.Zhang, and S. Malik. Chaff: Engineering an efficient SAT solver. In *Proceedings of the 38th International Design Automation Conference - DAC 2001*, pages 530–535. ACM, 2001.

[Mon74]   U. Montanari. Networks of constraints: Fundamental properties and applications to picture processing. *Information Sciences*, 7:95–132, 1974.

[MOQ11]   D. Mehta, B. O'Sullivan, and L. Quesada. Value ordering for finding all solutions: Interactions with adaptive variable ordering. In *Proceedings of the 17th International Conference on Principles and Practice of Constraint Programming - CP 2011*, volume 6876 of *Lecture Notes in Computer Science*, pages 606–620. Springer, 2011.

[MS99]   J.P. Marques Silva. The impact of branching heuristics in propositional satisfiability algorithms. In *Proceedings of the 9th Portuguese Conference on Artificial Intelligence - EPIA 1999*, volume 1695 of *Lecture Notes in Computer Science*, pages 62–74. Springer, 1999.

[MSS96]   J. P. Marques Silva and K. A. Sakallah. GRASP - a new search algorithm for satisfiability. In *Proceedings of the International Conference on Computer-Aided Design - ICCAD 1996*, pages 220–227. ACM and IEEE Computer Society, 1996.

[NOT06]   R. Nieuwenhuis, A. Oliveras, and C. Tinelli. Solving SAT and SAT Modulo Theories: From an abstract Davis–Putnam–Logemann–Loveland procedure to DPLL(t). *Journal of the ACM*, 53(6):937–977, 2006.

[NSB$^+$07] N. Nethercote, P.J. Stuckey, R. Becket, S. Brand, G.J. Duck, and G. Tack. MiniZinc: Towards a standard CP modelling language. In *Proceedings of the 13th International Conference on Principles and Practice of Constraint Programming - CP 2007*, volume 4741 of *Lecture Notes in Computer Science*, pages 529–543. Springer, 2007. Software available at http://www.g12.cs.mu.oz.au/minizinc/download.html.

[PD09]   K. Pipatsrisawat and A. Darwiche. On the power of clause-learning SAT solvers with restarts. In *Proceedings of the 15th International Conference on Principles and Practice of Constraint Programming - CP 2009*, volume 5732 of *Lecture Notes in Computer Science*, pages 654–668. Springer, 2009.

[PJ97]   J.K. Pearson and P. Jeavons. A survey of tractable constraint satisfaction problems. Technical Report CSD-TR-97-15, Royal Holloway, University of London, 1997.

[Pre09]   S.D. Prestwich. CNF encodings. In A. Biere, M. Heule, H. van Maaren, and T. Walsh, editors, *Handbook of Satisfiability*, pages 75–97. IOS Press, 2009.

[Pro93]   P. Prosser. Hybrid algorithms for the constraint satisfaction problem. *Computational Intelligence*, 9(3):268–299, 1993.

[PSW00]   P. Prosser, K. Stergiou, and T. Walsh. Singleton consistencies. In *Proceedings of the 6th International Conference on Principles and Practice of Constraint Programming - CP 2000*, volume 1894 of *Lecture Notes in Computer Science*, pages 353–368. Springer, 2000.

[Pug05]   J.-F. Puget. Automatic detection of variable and value symmetries. In *Proceedings of the 11th International Conference on Principles and Practice of Constraint*

                Programming - CP 2005, volume 3709 of *Lecture Notes in Computer Science*, pages 475–489. Springer, 2005.

[QGLOvB05] C.-G. Quimper, A. Golynski, A. López-Ortiz, and P. van Beek. An efficient bounds consistency algorithm for the global cardinality constraint. *Constraints*, 10(2):115–135, 2005.

[RD00] I. Rish and R. Dechter. Resolution versus search: Two strategies for SAT. *Journal of Automated Reasoning*, 24(1–2):225–275, 2000.

[RDP91] F. Rossi, V. Dhar, and C.J. Petrie. On the equivalence of constraint satisfaction problems. In *Proceedings of the 9th European Conference on Artificial Intelligence - ECAI 1990*, pages 550–556. Pitman, 1991.

[Rég94] J.-C. Régin. A filtering algorithm for constraints of difference in CSPs. In *Proceedings of the 12th National (US) Conference on AI - AAAI 1994*, volume 1, pages 362–367. AAAI Press / The MIT Press, 1994.

[Rob65] J.A. Robinson. A machine-oriented logic based on the resolution principle. *Journal of the ACM*, 12(1):23–41, 1965.

[RS86] N. Robertson and P.D. Seymour. Graph Minors II. Algorithmic aspects of tree width. *Journal of Algorithms*, 7:309–322, 1986.

[Sab05] A. Sabharwal. SymChaff: A structure-aware satisfiability solver. In *Proceedings of the 20th National Conference on Artificial Intelligence and the Seventeenth Innovative Applications of Artificial Intelligence Conference - AAAI 2005*, pages 467–474. AAAI Press / The MIT Press, 2005.

[SB06] C. Sinz and A. Biere. Extended resolution proofs for conjoining BDDs. In *Proceedings of the 1st International Computer Science Symposium in Russia - CSR 2006*, volume 3967 of *Lecture Notes in Computer Science*, pages 600–611. Springer, 2006.

[SBdG$^+$08] M. Sanchez, S. Bouveret, S. de Givry, F. Heras, P. Jégou, J. Larrosa, S. Ndiaye, E. Rollon, T. Schiex, C. Terrioux, G. Verfaillie, and M. Zytnicki. Max-CSP competition 2008: Toulbar2 solver description. In *Proceedings of the 3rd International CSP Solver Competition*, pages 63–70, 2008.

[Sch78] T.J. Schaefer. The complexity of satisfiability problems. In *Proceedings of the 10th Annual ACM Symposium on Theory of Computing - STOC 1978*, pages 216–226. ACM, 1978.

[Sch11] C. Schulte. Gecode: An open constraint solving library. Presented at *Dagstuhl Seminar: Constraint Programming meets Machine Learning and Data Mining*, 2011. Software available at http://www.gecode.org/.

[SF94] D. Sabin and E.C. Freuder. Contradicting conventional wisdom in constraint satisfaction. In *Proceedings of the 2nd International Workshop on Principles and Practice of Constraint Programming - PPCP 1994*, volume 874 of *Lecture Notes in Computer Science*, pages 10–20. Springer, 1994.

[Sin05] C. Sinz. Towards an optimal CNF encoding of Boolean cardinality constraints. In *Proceedings of the 11th International Conference on Principles and Practice of Constraint Programming - CP 2005*, volume 3709 of *Lecture Notes in Computer Science*, pages 827–831. Springer, 2005.

[SLM92] B. Selman, H.J. Levesque, and D.G. Mitchell. A new method for solving hard satisfiability problems. In *Proceedings of the 10th National (US) Conference on Artificial Intelligence - AAAI 1992*, pages 440–446. AAAI Press / The MIT Press, 1992.

[SV93] T. Schiex and G. Verfaillie. Nogood recording for static and dynamic constraint satisfaction problems. In *Proceedings of the 5th International Conference on Tools with Artificial Intelligence - ICTAI 1993*, pages 48–55. IEEE Computer Society, 1993.

[SW99] K. Stergiou and T. Walsh. Encodings of non-binary constraint satisfaction problems. In *Proceedings of the 16th National (US) Conference on Artificial Intelligence - AAAI 1999, and Eleventh Conference on Innovative Applications of*

Artificial Intelligence - IAAI 1999, pages 163–168. AAAI Press / The MIT Press, 1999.

[Tsa93]   E. Tsang. *Foundations of constraint satisfaction*. Computation in cognitive science. Academic Press, 1993.

[TTKB09]   N. Tamura, A. Taga, S. Kitagawa, and M. Banbara. Compiling finite linear CSP into SAT. *Constraints*, 14(2):254–272, 2009. Software available at http://bach.istc.kobe-u.ac.jp/sugar/.

[vDLR06]   M.R.C. van Dongen, C. Lecoutre, and O. Roussel. Second international CSP solver competition. Instances and results available at http://www.cril.univ-artois.fr/CPAI06/, 2006.

[vDLR08]   M.R.C. van Dongen, C. Lecoutre, and O. Roussel. Third international CSP solver competition. Instances and results available at http://www.cril.univ-artois.fr/CPAI08/, 2008.

[vDLR09]   M.R.C. van Dongen, C. Lecoutre, and O. Roussel. Fourth international CSP solver competition. Instances and results available at http://www.cril.univ-artois.fr/CPAI09/, 2009.

[vHDT92]   P. van Hentenryck, Y. Deville, and C-M. Teng. A generic arc-consistency algorithm and its specializations. *Artificial Intelligence*, 57(2–3):291–321, 1992.

[Wal00]   T. Walsh. SAT v CSP. In *Proceedings of the 6th International Conference on Principles and Practice of Constraint Programming - CP 2000*, volume 1894 of *Lecture Notes in Computer Science*, pages 441–456. Springer, 2000.

[ŽJ10]   S. Živný and P. Jeavons. Classes of submodular constraints expressible by graph cuts. *Constraints*, 15(3):430–452, 2010.

[ZM02]   L. Zhang and S. Malik. The quest for efficient Boolean satisfiability solvers. In *Proceedings of the 14th International Conference on Computer Aided Verification - CAV 2002*, volume 2404 of *Lecture Notes in Computer Science*, pages 17–36. Springer, 2002.

[ZMMM01]   L. Zhang, C.F. Madigan, M.W. Moskewicz, and S. Malik. Efficient conflict driven learning in Boolean satisfiability solver. In *Proceedings of the 2001 International Conference on Computer-Aided Design - ICCAD 2001*, pages 279–285. ACM, 2001.

[ZS00]   H. Zhang and M.E. Stickel. Implementing the Davis-Putnam method. *Journal of Automated Reasoning*, 24(1–2):277–296, February 2000.

Printed in the United States
By Bookmasters